RODDY LLEWELLYN's
Gardening Year

Roddy Llewellyn

First published in Great Britain in 1997
by Metro Books (an imprint of Metro Publishing Limited),
19 Gerrard Street, London W1V 7LA

Some of the material in this book was previously
published in *Homes & Gardens* magazine.
Roddy Llewellyn is hereby identified as the author of
this work in accordance with Section 77 of the Copyright,
Designs and Patents Act 1988.

British Library Cataloguing in Publication Data. A CIP
record of this book is available on request from the British
Library.

ISBN 01 900512 28 9

10   9   8   7   6   5   4   3   2   1

Designed by Ivan Dodd Designers
Printed in Great Britain by Clays Ltd, St Ives, plc.

Contents

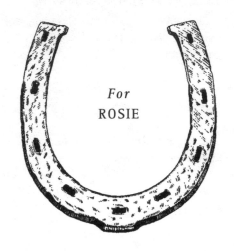

For
ROSIE

Introduction

It was a cold and wet January day when Tania and I first saw the old house, a pub which dates back to the fourteenth century. It was love at first sight: the sagging beams, the old stone, the ingle-nook fireplaces and oh! the view which stretches some forty miles to the Lambourne Downs.

The feeling was right. We knew straight away that it was just the house for us and our three daughters, Alexandra, Natasha and Rosie, who were then 12, 10 and 7 years old. At long last we felt we could put down roots, having led a semi-nomadic existence, this being our seventh move since we were married in 1981.

Half the attraction of the place was the adjoining land: nothing enormous, a neglected plot of about one acre on three sides of the house. This was just the right size for someone like me who spends his time designing and writing about other people's gardens, with only precious snatched moments and weekends to work on his own. The existing soil was in good shape, there were no serious weed infestations and, most important of all, it had enormous potential.

This is the story of how I set about developing that potential. It is a month-by-month diary of my first year in the garden and tells how, in September — the month we moved into our new home — I took stock of my neglected plot and thought about how I would turn it into my dream garden: how I wanted it to look and feel, the ways in which I and my family would want to use it and how I would achieve those objectives. After that, the hard work began!

However, this book is more than just the tale of my personal struggle with excavating machines, irrigation systems and cesspits. Anyone — no matter how large or tiny their plot — can, with careful planning and a little hard work, turn a neglected wilderness into the garden of their dreams; in the following pages, alongside the details of my own emerging garden, I offer practical advice and tips on how you can plan, plant and build your own outdoor space. I hope you will be inspired — as I was — to create a garden that will give you pleasure and satisfaction for years to come.

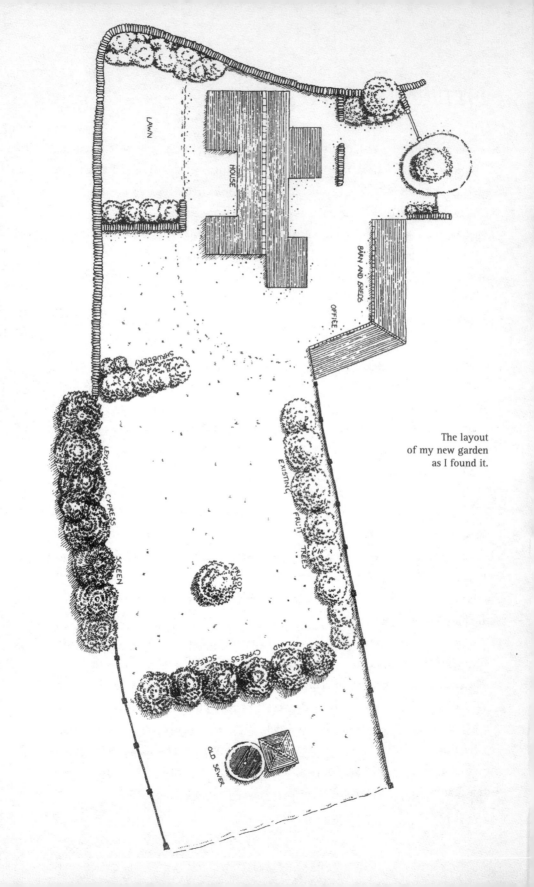

LAWN

HOUSE

SYCAMORE

BARN AND SHEDS

OFFICE

SHRUBBERY

LEYLAND CYPRESS SCREEN

EXISTING FRUIT TREES

APRICOT

LEYLAND CYPRESS SCREEN

OLD SEWER

The layout
of my new garden
as I found it.

Starting from scratch

SEPTEMBER

I N MY NEW GARDEN there are five separate areas to tackle from scratch. The largest, about a quarter of an acre, has the most potential and consists at present of a glorious mess of brambles, nettles, bindweed, stone dumps, broken fences and, worst of all, thirty-one 20m (60ft) tall Leyland cypresses. There are assorted fruit trees, apple trees, hazelnuts and one beautifully shaped apricot, but their bark has been badly nibbled by two 'rescued' donkeys which I allowed a neighbour to keep here because they had nowhere else to go. I feel I should have been better rewarded for my public-spiritedness. Luckily, the apricot escaped with little injury.

The apricot tree stood in the centre of the garden towards the far end and I soon realized its potential as an effective vista-stopper, especially if I painted its trunk and some of the lower branches with a white organic paint to make it stand out even more. Looking back towards the house from the apricot tree, I decided to establish the other end of this vista on a wall of the house, a sixties addition we affectionately refer to as the 'public lavatory' as it is rather square and ugly. I will eventually have painted on this wall, or attached to it, an eye-catching feature. A mirrored arch, perhaps, or a painted obelisk? The most important initial ingredient, the backbone, of this garden is thus established: a vista with eye-catching features at either end.

Starting at the apricot in my garden here, a six-foot wide passage opens up to a round lawn 13m (41ft) in diameter, before it once more returns to become a passage leading towards the focal point on the 'public lavatory'. I want the round lawn to remain uncluttered, stark even, consisting only of lawn and hedge, with the addition of a central pond whose exact shape and size I have not finally decided on yet, although it will be formal, of that I am certain.

GARDEN 'ROOMS'

Off this circle, through gaps in the hedge, I am planning a series of smaller, more informal gardens, separated from one another by hedges. After years of planning gardens I have come to the conclusion that it is asking too much to expect a whole garden, or even a bed or a border, to look wonderful all the year round. These additional gardens leading off from the circular lawn will be planted so that they perform at different times of the year.

I suppose I was influenced by Vita Sackville-West's treatment of her gardens at Sissinghurst when it comes to this 'compartmentalization', the art of using hedging to separate visually one part of the garden from another. The mixture of formality (clipped hedges and topiary) and informality (lax shrubs and trees and herbaceous plants) is always very pleasing.

Several ideas have already come to mind, the most obvious being a winter garden, with winter-flowering bulbs as well as cherries, wintersweet and witch hazel, shrubs with berries that last and plants with decorative seed heads.

I think I will choose one of the larger spaces for my winter garden, as there are so many deserving candidates. Trees will include common witch hazel (*Hamamelis mollis*), whose clear, yellow flowers I prefer to those of varieties like *Hamamelis* x *intermedia* – its muddy yellow flowers remind me of tired mustard – and the winter-flowering cherry, *Prunus* x *subhirtella* 'Autumnalis', whose white flowers appear during mild spells in winter.

Two obvious shrub choices for the winter garden are Sweet Box (*Sarcococca hookeriana*), with its deliciously scented, small, white flowers, and *Viburnum* x *bodnantense* 'Charles Lamont', whose pink flowers are slightly fuller and have the reputation of standing up better to winter wet than the ubiquitously cultivated 'Dawn'. Perhaps I shall try growing the fragrantly flowering shrub wintersweet (*Chimonanthus praecox*) and the winter-flowering honeysuckle (*Lonicera* x *purpusii*) out in the open, trained up cane tripods? I have only ever seen them trained up walls, but it is worth a try.

I intend to underplant the trees and shrubs with winter aconites (*Aconitum*), snowdrops (*Galanthus*) and winter-flowering cyclamen (*cyclamen coum*) – and I must have *Iris unguicularis*, which is so good in winter vases. I will plant a small group of them in a submerged black pot full of well-drained, poor soil – which is what they like best – as near as possible to the base of one of the south-facing hedges, for protection.

My garden will not include winter-flowering heathers. Somehow, they look out of place in domestic gardens. Heather is the only plant I can think of that is better off being left where it belongs – on the moor.

Other garden 'room' ideas I am planning include a late-summer-flowering garden, a rose garden, an outdoor dining room and a garden solely devoted to flowers for picking, so there is a lot more to think about.

Plans for the north side

Beyond the northern side of the circle of lawn, I intend adding more trees to complement the existing apples and filberts, the latter being the smart cousins of the hazelnuts. A fruit and nut garden, in effect. The first trees to come to mind are my favourites, the common mulberry (*Morus nigra*), good old reliable Victoria plum and a walnut (*Juglans*). They can later be underplanted with wild flowers and beautiful Turk's-cap lilies (*Lilium martagon*), that thrive in dappled shade.

SEPTEMBER

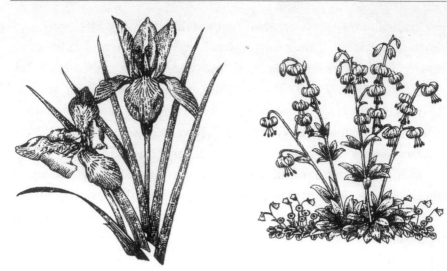

Iris unguicularis: an excellent cut flower.   *Lilium martagon* thrives in dappled shade.

I am not going to devote too much space to wild flowers for a number of reasons. My soil is quite rich and this is a disadvantage if you want to grow a wide range of them. I went to a lecture given by Rosemary Verey and the Prince of Wales on the gardens at Highgrove and they both pointed out that if your soil is too good, grasses take over almost completely. About the only robust and healthy survivors are ox-eye daisies. The only way I could get round this problem would be to scrape off the topsoil. I am not prepared to do this because I have a lovely, two-foot layer of friable top soil before I hit underlying clay and this would make the ground levels look very peculiar, as well as being a waste of good soil.

The south-facing garden

The south-facing back garden does not need much doing to it. It consists mostly of a lawn ending in a low stone wall. Beyond is the ravishing view of the Windrush Valley and beyond to the Lambourne Downs. Fussy landscaping would merely detract from it. It would be lovely to build a ha-ha here, as the steep-sided ditch would keep the rabbits out without interrupting the view; but this is an expensive operation and I fear it will only happen if I win the lottery.

I am planning a conservatory on this side of the house and I will enlarge and replant the existing border with silver, grey and white plants, a cooling mixture to suit forecasted warmer summers. I may even edge it in dwarf box (*Buxus sempervirens* 'Suffruticosa').

The small garden on the other side of the wall behind the silver and white border consists mostly of lawn and, in time, I want to link the two gardens via a gate.

This will entail bashing a hole through the wall and I am planning a gate to look like a cobweb, complete with gruesome-looking spider about to pounce on a trapped fly. I want it in iron, painted white and I shall soon have to start saving for it, but I am prepared to pay over the odds for something my heart desires rather than settling for an off-the-peg gate of little character.

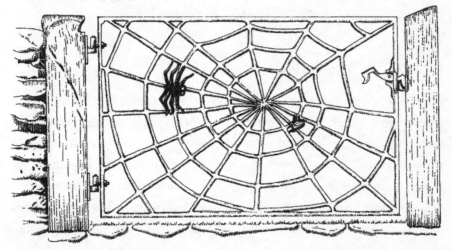

This is my idea for an unusual 'cobweb' gate.

At the far end of this small garden are the remains of an old shrubbery. The existing shrubs are rather pedestrian and are in desperate need of attention as they are all flopping into one another. There is a mixture of Forsythia, Philadelphus and winter-flowering Viburnums, with one saving glory, a tree peony with yellow flowers (*Paeonia delavayi* var. *ludlowii*). I will uproot half of them with the JCB and then thin, cut back and feed the remainder. Later, I can add some new, exciting inmates.

SEPTEMBER ❖

In this space, I want to establish another circle, the simplest and best of all geometric shapes, in order to destroy the straight lines of this rectangular garden. Around the edge of a circular lawn I am planning to grow the sort of herbs, flowers and vegetables that are so expensive in the shops. My initial list includes rocket, sweet peas, globe artichokes and rhubarb, the latter two having the advantage of ornamental leaves as well.

I am not going to attempt the likes of brassicas (cabbages), carrots and potatoes which, by the time you have taken the trouble to sow, water, weed, protect from the countless pests that attack them, dig and clean them, you might as well buy cheap when they are in season. However, I do find spring cabbage, everlasting spinach and Brussels sprouts worth growing because they seldom seem to succumb to physiological problems or fall prey to insects.

In front of the house

The front of the house faces the village green, which is surrounded by period houses built of the local stone. Directly opposite the house and belonging to us, is a round piece of grass we call 'the egg'. At its centre is a messy clump of hacked-about sycamores which, this autumn, I aim to replace with a specimen tree – most likely the Hungarian oak (*Quercus frainetto*). Around its base I want to plant a big dollop of snowdrops. Nearer the house I am planning a formal box hedge and gravel garden.

BACK TO EARTH

All these are dreams of Utopia but there is lots of groundwork to do first. The large garden slopes will need levelling; I need to trench for a new drain, taps and the electric conduit for the pond in the circle; and I must move the compost heap. I am not looking forward to cutting down, up-rooting, sawing up, part-burning and part-shredding the thirty-one dreaded Leyland cypresses, replacing rotten fences or emptying an obsolete cesspool. What do you do with an old cesspool? Turn it into a pond? Fill it in? The good news is that my local JCB operator tells me that this entire operation (save the disposal of detritus) should not cost me an arm and a leg.

This is only what needs doing in the biggest garden (and there are bound to be further nasties lurking underground – there always are). There are three more to go! But I am having a lovely time. At last I have the opportunity to plant a garden from scratch, for posterity. This has been a long-felt want.

 SEPTEMBER

LORD WARDINGTON'S DAMSON GIN

Autumn is the time for damsons. Here is the most delicious recipe for damson gin. I hope you will try it and enjoy it as much as I do. You will need:

Large bottle or jar with lid (with a neck big enough
to fit the damsons in)
1 bottle gin
450g (1lb) damsons
1 tablespoon demerara sugar
1 dash almond essence

TIP: PRICKING DAMSONS

 I find the easiest way to prick damsons and sloes is to roll them on a spiked oasis (a flat metal base with spikes sticking up from it, used in flower arranging).

Prick the damsons all over to let out the flavour.
Put the damsons in the bottle or jar.
Pour in the gin.
Add sugar and almond essence.
Lord Wardington suggests the addition of miniature bottle of Prunella de Bourgogne (French plum brandy).

A NEW GARDEN

Having moved to a new house and finding themselves with a garden, of whatever size, to play with, many people's impulse is to rush down to the garden centre and buy lots of lovely (and expensive) plants. This is like setting out on a journey without a road map and, more often than not, leads to chaos, with little hope of a harmonious, balanced garden emerging.

If you want to create a good garden, you need to draw up a proper garden plan, in scale. I shall show you how to do this in detail in the next chapter but, before you even think of putting pencil to paper, you need to think hard about your options and what you really want in your garden. I also advise living with the garden through all four seasons first, if you have the patience, to see what treasures emerge. For example, a garden first seen looking straggly in summer may contain wonderful displays of spring bulbs hidden from sight underground. Use this waiting time to think, plan and develop ideas. Some of the things you can do are:

❀ Look at what grows well in your neighbours' gardens for clues about the local soil and conditions.
❀ Note the names of plants you admire in gardens you visit. Ask their names and look up in books whether they are suitable for your garden.
❀ Visit garden centres to look at plants at different seasons to see what's available — but do not buy!
❀ Look at practical and picture gardening books for inspiration.
❀ If you are really impatient to get some colour in your garden and cannot face waiting a whole year, plant some fast- and large-growing annuals, such as *Ricinus communis*, *Nicotiana sylvestris*, *cosmos* and *cleome*, in a small, cleared patch of garden, or in pots and tubs.

What kind of garden?

One of the most important things to do is try to decide what kind of garden you want. Do you simply want to create an attractive space with trees, shrubs and flowers or do you have any special uses in mind? Ask yourself questions like these:

❀ Would you like to create a haven for wildlife, with unmown grass, an informal pond and lots of plants to attract birds, butterflies and bees?
❀ Do you want to have friends and family around for barbecues and informal parties outside? In this case, you might want as large a paved area as you can manage.
❀ Do you have young children? They like a big lawn to play on and you need to beware of water and poisonous plants and berries.
❀ Would a low-maintenance garden suit you? Busy people can plan to have plants that require no regular attention, plus large areas of lawn or paving, to cut right back on the work that needs doing.

Thinking about structure

While you are in this pondering, planning stage, try to decide on the basic structure of your garden design. For instance, I mentioned that my apricot tree was in just the right position to form a vista-stopper, or focal point, at the farthest edge of the garden from the house and that an imagined line between tree and house would form the backbone of my garden around which all the rest would be constructed.

Try to establish a similar backbone to base your own garden around. What you are aiming for is to find a vista – that's the longest view you can get from a much-used window or door overlooking the garden to the furthest edge of your boundary. A vista-stopper is just that, something interesting for your eyes to notice and be drawn to at the end of this long view. There may be something you could use as a vista-stopper more or less in position already (a tree, a rose arch or a paved area). If not, start thinking about what you might like to use. It need not be anything expensive; here are some ideas:

❀ **SEPTEMBER**

❀ A nicely shaped tree (emphasize it by painting the trunk and lower branches white with organic paint).

❀ A statue — the smaller the statue, the further away it looks, so you can create an optical illusion of distance.

❀ An arch — covered with roses, clematis or other climbers.

❀ A large pot on a plinth — you could plant it with flowers.

Just because you have a small garden, do not think you cannot establish a vista.

Some ideas for vista-stoppers.

In a small, rectangular town garden you may not have much choice of vistas, but you can still decide on a focal point at the far end of the garden and shape the rest of the space around it. In a more irregularly shaped garden, you may have several possible vistas.

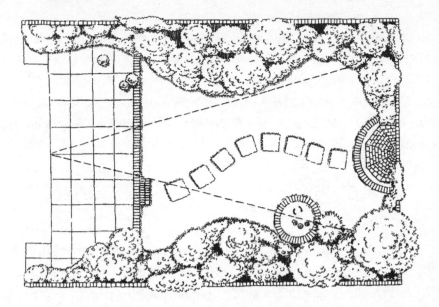

Here, two possible vistas are diagonals either side of the central summer house.

In this irregularly shaped garden, there are several possible vistas.

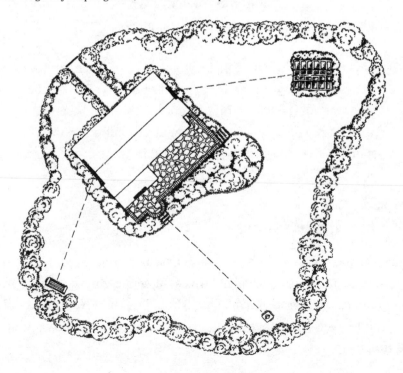

PAINTING A MURAL

To complete your backbone, or vista, it is a good idea to have a vista-stopper at the house end too, to attract your eye back when you are at the far end of the vista. A striking or colourful plant on the house wall would work, for example, or pots of flowers outside the door.

As I said, I am thinking of using a mural as my vista-stopper on the house wall. It is a fairly ambitious project, not for the complete beginner, but if you feel artistic and have a blank wall, there is no reason not to try it.

TIPS: MURALS AND MIRRORS

❀ To paint a mural, first make sure the wall is protected from rising damp by a damp-proof course and then cement-render to establish a smooth surface. Apply a masonry stabilizer and then a coat of white masonry paint. Use good-quality oil paints for the artwork and seal the whole with artist's oil varnish. (Acrylic paints and varnish can also be used, but oil paint lasts longer.) Each treatment must be allowed to dry before the next is applied.

❀ If you wish to use mirrors in your garden, remember that heavy-duty mirrors should be used outdoors. Protect the silvering on the back with bitumastic paint and then tape the edges with insulating tape. As a precaution against damage to birds, stretch fine netting in front of the mirror.

Fleshing out the bones

Once you have decided where your vista/backbone should go, start thinking about the other elements that will shape your garden: flower beds, borders, lawn, a pond and so on. Think in broad strokes — detailed planning of each element comes later. Here are some questions to help you think:

❦ Where do you want your main flower bed or beds? Is there a suitable wall or path to put a border along?

❦ Do you really want a lawn? It may seem an odd question, but a lawn in a very small garden can be hardly worth the bother of mowing. Using the space for paving, gravel or larger flower beds can work better. If you decide you do want a lawn, see page 14.

❦ Do you want a greenhouse? Before you decide, think carefully about whether you will really use one – they take up a fair bit of space and are expensive.

❦ Will you need a shed? Think carefully again. They can be quite an eyesore and you may be able to fit your garden tools in a garage, or even in the house.

❦ Are you planning a conservatory? Will it be a true conservatory for growing plants or simply a wonderful, sunny glass room for sitting in? See the tips on page 14 for a plant conservatory.

❦ Would you like a pond? It is possible to make ponds even in small spaces (see page 138). But remember the dangers of water to small children – ponds are best avoided until the children are older.

❦ Will you need paths, pergolas, walls or hedges to help you reach parts of the garden, or help divide it up? Remember, all of these elements cost money – quite a lot of it, sometimes – so calculate the price before deciding to plant yards of exotic hedging. This is another reason to do a scale plan (see page 30). There is more about compartmentalizing a garden on page 16.

❦ Trees make a big difference to a garden. Will you plant some? Or do you have too many crowding your space? Even the tiniest garden can support dwarf trees to give interesting shapes.

❦ Do you feel the need for a fruit and vegetable garden? It takes up a lot of space and is hard work, too. Consider integrating fruit and veg into the rest of the garden. Put vegetables and salads in a parterre or potager (see page 22). Fruit trees can be trained up sunny walls. Globe artichokes, asparagus, tree onions and other vegetables that look ornamental can be included in a border. Grow herbs in pots outside the kitchen door or include them in borders.

SEPTEMBER ❀

TIPS: CONSERVATORIES

The five most important considerations when planning a conservatory are:

❀ Underfloor heating: either using hot pipes under ducts or warming cable laid under the floor. This gives a much more even heat than radiators, which is better for plants.

❀ A paved floor: so you never have to worry when you spill water. Dampened floors during very hot weather result in higher humidity levels, something that plants relish.

❀ Shading: conservatories can become uncomfortably hot in mid-summer, so some sort of shading (such as blinds) is necessary, especially if the building faces south.

❀ Vents or windows: at the highest point to release excess heat and insects.

❀ Planning permission: may be necessary.

A NEW LAWN

The best month to sow seed or lay turf (sowing is very much cheaper) for a new lawn is September, usually a wettish month when there is still some warmth in the ground, resulting in good germination. By the time winter comes along the grass has got its roots down resulting in a head start the following spring and a usable lawn the following July. At first there seem to be many more weeds than grass. This is nothing to worry about as successive mowings will strengthen the grass at the expense of the weeds. An application of selective weed-killer is not always necessary.

Sowing

Seeding a lawn is made all the easier these days as leading seed merchants offer a range of seed to suit different conditions. You can get seed mixes for football pitches as well as for difficult places under trees. So long as you have an average, well-drained soil you can achieve a good-looking lawn without any trouble. There is nothing difficult about it so long as the ground is made as flat as possible and the surface is raked clean of surface stones before sowing or turfing.

Turfing

The best time to turf is also September although it can be laid any time during the winter so long as the ground is not frozen or waterlogged. Do not leave it much after early April just in case a long dry summer follows, resulting in dead patches, although you will be surprised at how well it bounces back in a wet autumn.

TIP: BUYING TURF

 Always inspect turf on the lorry before it has been unloaded to see if it is of sufficiently good quality (that is, not full of weeds). Turf comes in varying qualities; if you settle for the cheapest you must expect the occasional weed.

THE THINGS YOU FORGET

In your musings about your garden plan, do not forget to give some thought to the more mundane things that are easy to forget, such as:

✿ Washing line: Do you need one up permanently? Build a screen to hide a whirly-gig style line, or use a spring-loaded one that pulls out from the wall when required and disappears when not needed.

SEPTEMBER ❃

❃ Taps: It is really useful to have an outside tap in any garden. For a small garden, a tap attached to the house wall outside a kitchen or lavatory by a plumber is probably fine. Ask for it to be installed with an inner stop-cock so it can be turned off outside in winter, to stop it from freezing and bursting. For larger gardens, it makes sense to have a tap at the far end, but this means laying pipes. If you can do this while carrying out major reconstruction in the garden, I would certainly recommend it.

❃ Lighting: This is not most people's first consideration when planning a garden, but lighting makes all the difference, especially in winter. Whether you simply want a light on the house wall so you can see to get to the dustbin, floodlights to bathe a drive or expanse of lawn in light, or individual spotlights for features such as statues or a bench, plan them in at this stage and investigate the costs and the logistics of installing them.

A GARDEN FOR ALL SEASONS

If my plan of creating garden 'rooms' appeals to you, but you have limited space, you can adapt the idea and still plan areas that perform at different times of the year. I do not suggest that the entire garden should become a series of separate compartments but if you create a garden where some parts are not immediately visible, it adds an element of mystery and surprise and also makes the garden seem larger than it is in reality.

An added advantage of having 'walls' round your garden 'rooms' is that you do not have to look at them when they are not at their best. A spring garden in summer and a late summer garden in winter have nothing to offer, for example and are better hidden. The aim is to plan self-contained areas to look their best at a certain time of year, without worrying that they are less spectacular at other times, which is always a concern in an open garden.

As all gardens are different there is no simple formula to follow for planning rooms like these; the best way is to decide how many separate areas you can logically include when you draw your scale plan. Here are a few guidelines:

❀ You can make your rooms irregular shapes and sizes, or all the same.
❀ Try to use any existing elements, such as a hedge, path or rose arch as natural dividers.
❀ Take into account whether the space is shaded or sunny and which way it faces, when you decide what sort of garden you will plant there.

CREATING 'WALLS'

In a large garden, you can use hedges, such as beech or yew, to divide the garden rooms. They need to be at least 60cm (2ft) wide and be careful to ensure that you are able to reach both sides of them easily for clipping.

In a small garden, where every inch counts, the walls of the rooms will need to be thinner. You could try using 2m (6ft) tall feather-board wooden fence, stained quite dark. This way you get your divisions instantly. If you plant common green ivy (*Hedera helix*), a neat, self-clinging climber that does not bush out too much, every 60cm (2ft) or so along the base, it should fully clothe the fencing within about seven years. Do not use fancy varieties of ivy with variegated leaves. They will not give the desired impression of a green hedge. Once the ivy reaches the top of the fence, it will need trimming whenever it starts to look shaggy.

Plan paths and stepping stones within the gardens so that all parts are accessible for easy maintenance.

IDEAS FOR GARDEN ROOMS

Now comes the exciting part. What will you plant in the rooms? Here are just a few of my ideas.

❀ SEPTEMBER

A fern garden

Some people think ferns are difficult to grow, but if you have a damp or shaded area it will give ferns the conditions they enjoy and they should flourish. You will need some evergreen ferns to prolong the 'high season' in your fern garden but the garden can also sport some of the rarer ferns, which often die down in winter. Some especially decorative ferns to try are:

Matteuccia struthiopteris (Shuttlecock fern)
Dryopteris dilatata (Broad buckler fern)
Athyrium filix-femina 'Frizelliae'

Good evergreen ferns are:

Polystichum setiferum (Soft shield fern) and varieties of it
(*P. s. divisilobum* is particularly attractive because of its graceful,
  lax fronds, for example).
Polypodium (Common polypody) and its varieties, of which *P. vulgare*
  'Cornubiense Grandiceps', with frothy, deeply-cut fronds is
  generally considered to be one of the most handsome.

A late summer garden

Since gardens often look tired by August and September, with bedraggled perennials and shrubs past their best, it seems a good idea to devote one of the rooms to plants that come into their own at that time. This gives you the opportunity to mix plants which have flowers of clear or dirty yellow, red and orange, as well as those with purple foliage. Isolated in a mixed border, these plants, especially those with russety hues, can look alien, whereas massed together they make a breathtaking display. This combination was loved by the Victorians, a fashion that has not yet returned in the cyclical nature of things – perhaps its time has come again.

SEPTEMBER

There are a great many late-flowering plants to choose from. Here are a few of my favourites:

yellow *rudbeckias,* especially *R. maxima*
orange dahlias and day lilies
red *geums* and *crocosmias*
purple *Ricinus communis* and plantain
yellow *anthemis* and *kniphofia*
reddy-brown *Helenium autumnalis*

Just as Claude Monet used the common nasturtium to crawl over the path between his borders at Giverny, you can achieve the same effect using a variety with double red flowers, *Tropaeolum majus* 'Hermine Grashoff', which could be enticed to scramble among plants within the border. The Hot Border at West Dean Gardens, near Chichester in West Sussex, was my inspiration for this.

A scented garden

A garden that includes all the most famously scented plants is another alternative. Try shrubs such as:
Philadelphus 'Beauclerk'
Azara microphylla
Daphne odora 'Aureo-marginata'

with annuals in between, such as:
night-scented stocks (*Matthiola*) – these are particularly wonderful
    beneath a window.
flowering tobacco *(Nicotiana alata syn. N. affinis).*
sweet peas *(Lathyrus odoratus)* - train them up a tripod or obelisk.

The joy of a scented room is that the walls trap the scent, making it the perfect place to visit on a balmy evening when most scented flowers are at their peak. You could include winter-flowering shrubs in this garden if you do not have the space for a separate winter garden. Plant the following for glorious scent:

Christmas box (*Sarcococca hookeriana*)
Honeysuckle (*Lonicera* x *purpusii*)
Wintersweet (*Chimonanthus praecox*)

A picking garden

A picking border is a great luxury. In a small garden you may not have room for a whole bed, but it could be worth creating a small patch, away from the house. A specially-planted section means you never have to denude parts of the garden that are visible from the house. There are a great many plants whose flowers last well in a vase and a great many more whose flowers dry well for winter decoration. Here are some I consider to be the best:

FLOWERS FOR CUTTING
Agapanthus (African lily)
Alchemilla (Lady's mantle)
Allium (Ornamental onion)
Alstroemeria (Peruvian lily)
Asparagus
Aster, esp. *ericoides* (Michaelmas daisy)
Buddleja davidii (Butterfly bush) and varieties
Canna lily (Indian shot)
Centaurea cyanus (Cornflower)
Cheiranthus (Wallflower)
Chimonanthus (Wintersweet)
Chrysanthemum
Convallaria majalis (Lily of the valley)
Cortaderia (Pampas grass)
Cosmos
Cotinus (Smoke bush)

SEPTEMBER

Cynara (Globe artichoke)

Dahlia

Delphinium

Dianthus barbatus (Sweet William)

Dianthus (Pink)

Dictamnus (Leopard's bane)

Echinops (Globe thistle)

Eremurus (Foxtail lily)

Eryngium (Sea holly)

Garrya (Silk tassle bush)

Gladiolus

Kniphofia (Red hot poker)

Lathyrus (Sweet pea)

Matthiola (Stock)

Narcissus (Daffodil)

Philadelphus (Mock orange)

Rosa (Rose)

Syringa (Lilac)

Tulipa (Tulip)

✿ SEPTEMBER

FLOWERS FOR DRYING

Achillea (Yarrow)

Amaranthus paniculatus (Love-lies-bleeding)

Anethum graveolens (Dill)

Centaurea (Cornflower)

Dipsacus fullonum (Common teasel)

Helichrysum bracteatum (Strawflower)

Hydrangea

Iberis (Candytuft)

Lavandula (Lavender)

Nigella (Love-in-a-mist)

Physalis (Chinese lantern)

Santolina (Lavender cotton)

Solidago (Golden rod)

Humulus lupulus (Hop)

Grasses, many, including *Agrostis nebulosa* (Cloud grass),
   Pennisetum villosum (Feathertop grass), *Pennisetum setaceum*
   (Fountain grass)

Helianthus annuus (Sunflower)

Moluccella laevis (Bells of Ireland)

Sedum maximum (Ice plant)

INDIVIDUAL STYLE

My reference to denuding flowers that are visible from the house
reminds me of a leading garden designer and his own garden in the
country. David Hicks has laid out a very sculptural garden surrounding
his house, consisting of stilted horsechestnut and assorted hedging
and has planned it so that there is never *one* flower visible from any
window at any time of the year.

A parterre garden

A parterre is a formal garden arranged in patterns, often surrounded
by low hedges. This is a delightful idea for a small, square or rectangular garden room. Evergreen dwarf box (*Buxus sempervirens*
'Suffruticosa') is a popular choice for defining edges, as it can be
admired all year round. Straight, geometric shapes, such as squares
and rectangles are easiest, though you could try a circle, or more
flowing shapes. This may sound ambitious, but it is perfectly possible,
even with limited space. I've seen it done beautifully in a London
front garden about 3m (9ft) square.

   Plant the beds with either annual flowers or herbs. This will give
a spectacular show, with each section of the parterre devoted to one
colour of flowers or one herb only. Some suitable herbs are golden
marjoram, silver or golden thyme and green, purple or variegated
sage. These have attractive, contrasting leaves, flower prettily, are
compact and need little trimming – so your parterre is easy to care for.

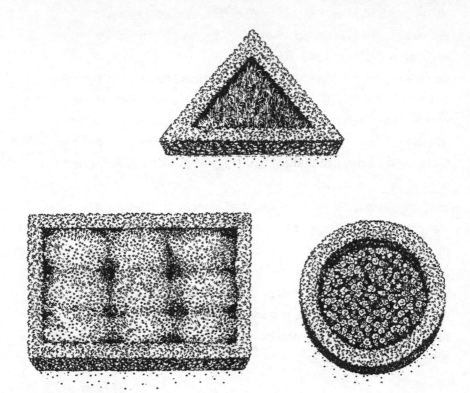

Some shapes for a parterre garden.

Low-maintenance gardens

A garden can be planted to minimize maintenance to suit those who work long hours, as well as those who want their garden to look good but who are not sufficiently interested in gardening to spend hours with trowel in hand. Although such planting will inevitably exclude many beautiful plants, it can still result in a masterpiece, needing just one clean-up in either spring or autumn. Here are some tips for low-maintenance gardening:

❀ Choose low-maintenance shrubs that do not need much attention, such as any of the junipers, azaleas and rhododendrons (acid soils only) and ornamental acers.

SEPTEMBER

SEPTEMBER

❁ In small gardens, lay paving or gravel instead of turf.

❁ Install automatic watering systems to suit your needs.

❁ Buy and do not grow veg or fruit.

❁ To avoid having to clear away the dead remains of spring flowering bulbs in early summer, interplant them with large-leaved herbaceous perennials. Daffodils interplanted with *Hosta sieboldiana* var. '*Elegans*' is a perfect example. By the time the daffodils die down, the leaves of the hostas hide them from sight, resulting in only one clear-up needed in the autumn.

❁ Plant trees. So long as they are planted where they can fully mature without competition from any other, they need no regular pruning, although they may need pruning a little in order to establish a good shape when they are young. After about ten years' growth, you can start removing lower branches to reveal the trunk.

❁ Keep weeding to a minimum by encouraging ground-cover plants to smother the ground, making it hard for weeds to grow. Here is a selection of some of the best:

GROUND-COVER PLANTS FOR SHADED AREAS

Epimediums

Euphorbia robbiae

Geranium phaeum; *G; sylvaticum*

Hedera canariensis 'Azorica' (ivy); *H. colchica*; *Hedera helix*
    (Common ivy)

Hypericum calycinum (St John's wort)

Pachysandra terminalis

Vinca (Periwinkle)

GROUND-COVER PLANTS FOR SUNNY AREAS

Ajuga reptans (Bugle)

Anthemis nobilis (Chamomile)

Bergenia (Elephant's ears)

Cerastium tomentosum (Snow in summer)

Geranium macrorrhizum 'Russell Prichard'

Hebe rakaiensis
Helianthemum (Rock rose)
Origanum vulgare 'Aureum' (Golden marjoram)
Stachys byzantina 'Silver Carpet' (Lamb's ears)
Tellima grandiflora 'Purpurea'
Thymus (Thyme)
Tiarella cordifolia (Foamflower)
Viola cornuta (Horned violet)

SEPTEMBER TASKS

❀ Plant daffodils – the sooner you get them in the better.

❀ It is easy to have a supply of fresh mint all winter on a sunny, warm kitchen window sill. All you have to do is to dig up some nice fat roots from the garden, cut them into 15cm (6in) lengths and lay them horizontally into a pot and cover them with about an inch of soil. New shoots will soon appear and cropping can start in about six weeks.

❀ This is a good month for planting all evergreens.

❀ Have you thought of building a bird table for those hungry birds in winter? (See page 101.)

❀ Prepare a simple compost bin of chicken wire for all those leaves about to fall. (See page 84.)

❀ Remove the shading on greenhouse glass and check all heating appliances to make sure they are working properly.

❀ Clean out gutters of dead moss and climbing plants.

❀ Bush roses should be reduced in height by about one-third to reduce damage to the roots in winter by wind rock.

❀ Rope onions together and hang them in a frost-free, cool place.

❀ Harvest globe artichokes before the purple flowers appear at their centre.

❀ Green tomatoes can be encouraged to ripen if put on a plate with an apple in a sunny window. The gas given off by the apple will help some of the tomatoes to ripen. The rest can be made into pickle.

Outdoor tomato varieties can be brought into the greenhouse in their pots where they are more likely to ripen.

❀ Replace any worn or damaged turves, or reseed.

SEPTEMBER ❀

First plans

OCTOBER

CLUNK! MY SPADE HIT SOMETHING HARD and quite large. As I dug round it gingerly, a white rim appeared. Another old ceramic sink for the collection. I now have five. I might plant one as a sink garden for the children; they like little alpines, along with special pebbles and shells brought back from summer holidays. I will probably sell the rest of the china sinks to help pay for some of the trees and shrubs I will be planting soon. The more I think about it, the more this seems a mammoth task I am taking on, involving considerable expense. I always tell clients to budget for the garden along with the house, but in this case I am not practising what I preach.

DENTED IDEALISM

I have decided to clobber most of the site for my new, big garden with systemic weedkiller. Half an acre is, after all, smothered in couch grass, nettles, thistles and docks (I am grateful I have no mare's tail or ground elder). I cannot even begin to envisage hand-digging such a large area twice over before I can plant, so a 'bare earth' policy seems to be the most practical solution.

I have come to the conclusion that I would have to be very rich to be a 100 per cent 'green' gardener — to clear the ground of weeds by hand, in this particular case. Yes, I do have the alternative of mulching the entire area with organic matter, then covering it with weighted-down heavy duty polythene and leaving it for a year, but I am too impatient and too lazy. I will be using glyphosate-based treatments which are rendered harmless on contact with the soil, so my conscience is clear.

MAYHEM AND DESTRUCTION

Well now, I have been having fun. The JCB has been doing its bit. Tim, the operator, looked as if he could have done the work by hand himself — he looks like a rugby scrum half. My surface water drain was installed in a jiffy and the concrete by the house torn up like sugar icing from a cake. I have just been told that I have to trench right back to my main stop-cock off the green in front of the house to install electric cable for the submersible pump and pipes for my irrigation system. Curses!

I have decided not to remove the thirty-one 60ft Leyland cypresses in their entirety, although I have every intention of killing them by removing all their foliage. I am going to remove every other one, leaving them as 10ft poles and then swag chain between them. If they look silly I can always remove them altogether. The JCB will take out the alternate trees which I have left as 3ft stumps.

AN IDEA FOR A HEDGE

My scale plan on paper, the best way to plan a garden of this complexity, is coming on a treat. Scale drawings leave little room for error when positioning plants and their other invaluable asset is that they allow you to work out as accurately as possible the amount of paving materials, turf, hedging, etc., that you need, by calculating measurements with a ruler. To date I have included 138m (450ft) of hedging, including yew and beech, my two favourites. I love the idea of a hedge with yew, purple beech, variegated holly and something yellow (but what?) to make patches of colour that blend together like a tapestry pattern; but the more I think about it, the more I veer towards a 'marble', as opposed to a 'tapestry' hedge. I shall have to ponder this and keep it a secret for the time being.

I will use beech, but I would have chosen hornbeam if my soil had been heavy clay, as it is far better suited to it. Beech and hornbeam have such similar leaves that it really makes little difference which one you plant, except that I have noticed that the persisting dead leaves on hornbeam become more raggedy as winter marches on. The only nuisance value of both plants is that they shed their old leaves in spring, but that is a small price to pay.

A LEGACY OF TREES

There are three common elders growing along the south side of the garden and they look pretty wretched after the long, hot summer — scanty leaves and few berries. This surprises me as they are extremely tough in every other respect. I have always thought the common elder a very underestimated tree. It is hardly ever planted as a 'garden tree' and I cannot understand why. Its large, flat, white flowers in May are both decorative and scented and the bees love them. The elderberries in autumn do not have the strength of flavour of the flowers, although they look as if they should somehow, but they are certainly decorative.

Elderflowers are both decorative and scented — bees love them.

I can only put the unpopularity of the elder down to the fact that it is generally considered to be a scrubby, hedgerow plant, altogether too common to contemplate in an ornamental setting. In southern Germany, however, where I have designed a number of gardens, the common elder features large in nursery catalogues; because their climate in winter is positively evil compared to ours, their choice of 'ornamental' trees is limited. So, what I have done is to shape some of my elders, taking out lower branches and dead wood as I go.

Apart from the apples and the one apricot in the large garden, I only inherited three other good trees: a weeping ash in the front, a damson and a small magnolia in the back garden.

THE BOUNDARY

The elder and its fellow country hedgemates, should be planted, I think, where garden meets farmland. I always feel that this boundary should be given more careful thought than is normally the case, so that one blends in with the other as far as possible. The prime example of what *not* to do along a country boundary is plant Leyland cypresses – in stiff, regimented rows they look completely out of context with the English countryside.

The year is advancing and frosts are threatening already – I must plant soon.

MAKING A GARDEN PLAN

It may seem a bit of an effort to do a proper plan of your garden, especially if you are eager to get started on it. However it is really the only way to create a well-structured garden including all the elements you require. The first thing you need to do is to measure your garden and mark all the existing features in it – this is the survey. Then you can plan out your new ideas and any changes you want to make – this is the plan.

The survey

Before you start your survey, decide what scale you will use. The scale of 1:5 is normally used for drawing features like pergolas and arches; 1:20 is suitable for a very small area like a balcony or a detailed swimming pool; 1:50 for a garden measuring about 15 x 10m (50 x 30ft); and 1:100 for gardens of about half an acre (0.2 hectares). Larger gardens are normally planned to a scale of 1:200 and 1:500 or 1:1000 are used for much larger areas of parkland or development. These large scales mean that there is little room for detail and therefore it sometimes proves necessary to draw a series of overlapping plans of 1:100.

A scale of 1:20 means that every unit on your drawing (each centimetre square on your graph paper, etc.) represents twenty of the same units in real life. For example, a flower bed measuring 3 x 4m is represented on paper as 15 x 20cm. Here's how to work this out:

$$(3m =) 300cm \times (4m =) 400cm$$
$$300 \div 20 = 15cm \times 400 \div 20 = 20cm$$

A scale rule helps you do the calculations. Use the edge marked with the scale you have chosen. Find where the actual distance in real life is marked in millimetres on the ruler (e.g., 300cm = 3000mm). Mark the distance (if you check with an ordinary ruler, the line will measure 15cm, as shown in the calculation above).

For the survey, you will need:

A small, light-weight table (for example, a collapsible
   picnic or card table), larger than your piece of graph paper
Graph paper 558 x 762mm (22 x 30in). This comes marked in
   different grids. I prefer one with 1, 5 and 10 squares on it.
Clips or weights to secure the paper onto the table
A scale rule which marks the scales 1:5, 1:20, 1:50, 1:100, 1:200,
   1:500 and 1:1000
A 30m (100ft) field tape; a pencil; an eraser; a compass.

OCTOBER ❖

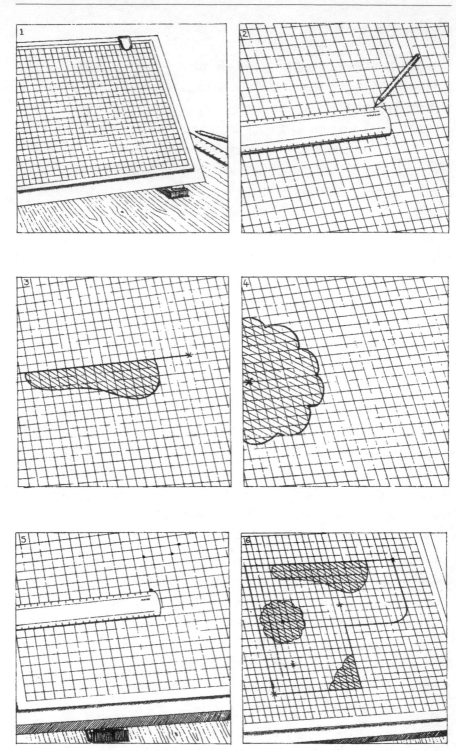

1.   Clip or weight the paper to the table. It is best to start with a long, straight line – a boundary fence, for example.

2.   Measure the line. Calculate and draw it to the correct scale on your graph paper. Use a scale rule and the grid lines to help you.

3.   With the tape still on the ground, measure and mark in scale where plants and features you want to keep are along this line.

4.   When you show trees, mark how far the branches spread, as you will need to know how much area is shaded beneath them.

5.   Now measure 90° from the first line across to the opposite boundary, at several points. Mark these widths and any features along the measure. Only mark features you want to keep, not those you will remove.

6.   Join the width marks to form the opposite boundary.

❦ OCTOBER

TIPS: SURVEYING

❀ It is a good idea to ask a friend to help. He can hold the other end of the tape and call out measurements.

❀ It is not worth buying specialist equipment for just your own garden. Ask around and see if you can borrow any of the equipment.

❀ Choose a calm, dry day.

❀ If you have a large garden with many existing features or radical ground-level changes, it is probably worth paying a surveyor to do it for you.

❀ Add the position of your house to the plan, showing windows and doors. Use the compass to find north and mark it on. If you know where north is, you can tell where shadows will fall at different times of day and which areas will be mainly sunny or shady so you can plan suitable plants and somewhere sunny to sit.

A scale rule will help with the calculations for your survey

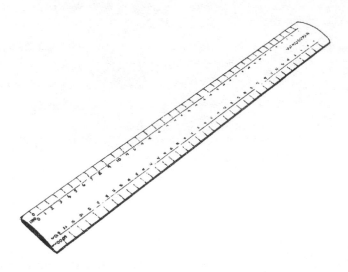

OCTOBER ❂

The plan

Once you have done your survey, you can start planning the changes and improvements you want to make, armed with all the notes and ideas you have prepared

The first step is to transfer the information from your survey onto fresh graph paper. To transfer the survey, you will need:

A large, stable flat surface to work on. An architect's drawing board is ideal, but a table will do.

A sheet of tracing paper big enough to fit over your survey. Sizes A2, A1 and A0 are available from good stationers.

A clean sheet of graph paper, as for the survey

2 HB pencils

An artist's or architect's pen. The size of nibs vary from 0.1 (the finest) to 0.8 (the thickest). I use 0.3 and 0.5 the most. Good art suppliers sell these, though you could use an ordinary, very fine, black pen if you prefer.

Scale rule, masking tape, a putty eraser

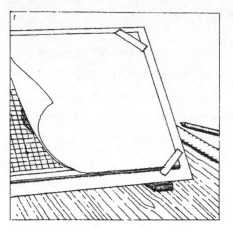

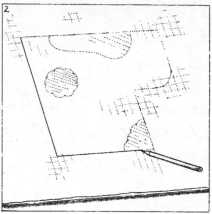

Secure your survey drawing onto your work surface with masking tape. Tape the tracing paper on top of it.

Trace the survey, showing the shape of the garden and the features you want to keep only. Transfer to graph paper.

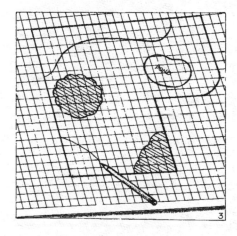

Draw in position all the features you want to change or add, such as a patio, lawn, pond, flower beds and paths.

✿ OCTOBER

Tree alert

Your garden plan may involve cutting down one or more trees. Be warned, trees may be protected by a Tree Preservation Order (TPO), particularly if they are of a certain age or a protected species. You can find out if they are from your local council and, if this proves to be the case, you will need to apply for permission before you touch them. Hefty fines can result if this is ignored.

Keeping to budget

Your garden plan is very useful for calculating the costs of materials. You can investigate the costs of various materials and work out exactly how much different options will cost, allowing you to stay within your budget. Do not be despondent if your first choice is too expensive, there are usually good options at a more reasonable rate.

OCTOBER ✿

LAYING PAVERS TO CREATE AN INTERESTING EFFECT.

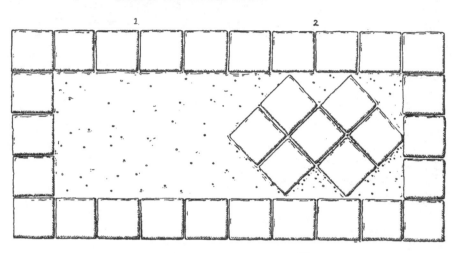

1. Frame the outside of the area to be paved with pavers laid end to end.

2. Fill in the centre with pavers set at a 45° angle or in a diamond pattern.

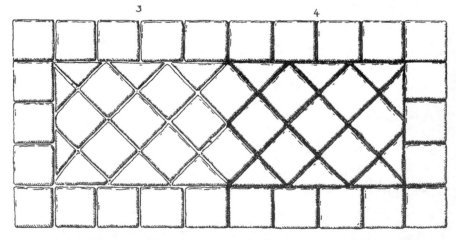

3. Cut pavers to fill in the spare spaces between the border and the middle.

4. Grout with cement of a complementary colour (e.g., dirty yellow with terracotta).

For example, quarried materials like York stone look really good but can be too expensive for the average budget. There are many good stone substitutes on the market now. Try moulded pavers of reconstituted cement with a natural-looking, riven finish. With a bit of imagination, even the cheapest materials can look good. The diagram opposite shows you how to make the most ordinary square pavers look special. It requires a certain amount of cutting, so you will need to hire a stone cutter, but the end result is well worth it. Another attractive alternative is to lay brick using patterns such as basket weave and herring bone.

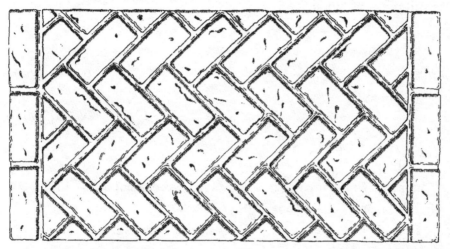

Bricks laid in a herringbone pattern.

Bricks laid in a basket weave pattern.

❀OCTOBER

The high-tech way?

If you feel that drawing a garden survey and plan is a rather laborious way of designing your garden, you may consider doing it by computer. There are now sophisticated computer programs to help you design gardens. If you are a computer whiz, by all means see if you can get hold of the technology and have a go.

From a professional point of view, I still believe the best way to plan a garden is by hand. I know that many garden architects have tried to design by computer but most have found that hand-drawing is still the best option.

I find my clients prefer a more personal touch and unless you are advanced in computer literacy the whole process takes much longer. Fine details that are added without effort by hand become cumbersome on a computer.

WEEDKILLERS

Weeding can be hard work. It is best to weed regularly – little and often is much easier to cope with.

Keep annual weeds in check by hoeing. This slices the roots off and they die. If hoeing is impractical because you have a huge area to treat, use 'contact' herbicides. They kill all the green parts of a plant that they touch.

For tough jobs, such as a large, weed-infested area, use a systemic or translocated weedkiller. Dilute it with water and spray it onto the green parts of tough, perennial weeds such as couch grass, docks, dandelion and thistle, which have pervasive and often deep root systems. It spreads through the plant's whole system right down to the roots and is best used when the plants are growing hard and fast in late spring. Serious infestations may need a second application. It is sold under a wide range of proprietorial names, but they all contain the one vital ingredient, a chemical called 'glyphosate', which is rendered harmless once it gets into contact with the soil. You will know that you're buying the right product if glyphosate is mentioned on the back of the bottle or packet.

Systemic herbicides kill every growing plant they touch. Only use it on a dry day and never when it is windy. It is safer to apply it with a 'dribble bar' attached to the end of a watering can's spout, as opposed to a pressure sprayer, as the droplets are heavier and therefore less likely to drift off and damage precious plants.

TREES

Planting a tree is a noble thing to do as you are contributing towards posterity. As you have seen, I am giving a lot of consideration to the trees I will plant in my garden.

Trees give all-important height and structure to a garden and are invaluable as screening plants. However, there are so many trees available that it is sometimes hard to decide what would be good for your garden. I have therefore included a list of some of the ones I think are the most rewarding. I am not including large forest trees like beech, oak and cedar but sticking to ornamental garden trees only.

All the trees included in this section are listed in the Royal Horticultural Society's 'Award of Garden Merit Plants'. This indicates that they are hardy, decorative, of good constitution, not particularly susceptible to pests and diseases, not requiring specialist care and are easily available.

> TIP: SOURCING PLANTS
>
> ❀ If you have difficulty sourcing a plant, *The RHS Plant Finder* (published by Dorling Kindersley Ltd, 9 Henrietta Street, London WC2E 8PS, available at comprehensive garden centres and bookshops) will find it for you. It lists over 70,000 plant names, from trees to alpines and the 700 nurseries that supply them.

OCTOBER

Here is a selection of my favourite garden ornamental trees:

D = Deciduous E = Evergreen H = eventual Height S = eventual
Spread. Measurements will vary according to the site and location of
the tree.

Acer platanoides 'Drummondii' (Variegated Norway maple) D H25m
 (82ft) S15m (50ft). This is the largest tree in this section, but I felt
 I had to include it for its beautiful bright green leaves broadly
 edged in creamy white.

Acer grosseri var. *hersii* (Snake bark maple) D H10m (30ft) S10m
 (30ft). This tree is famous for its wonderfully ornamental bark,
 with white stripes covering its trunk and branches. Good autumn
 colour.

Acer shirasawanum 'Aureum' D H10m (30ft) S10m (30ft). Probably the
 most beautiful of all the ornamental japanese acers, with rounded,
 rich yellow leaves. 'Aconitifolium' and 'Vitifolium' are also very
 good value. Slow growing and requires shelter from strong winds.

Acer palmatum 'Senkaki' D H4.5m (15ft) S4.5m (15ft). A tree for
 winter decoration with bright pink/red young twigs. Good yellow
 autumn tints which complement the red twigs. Note: Acers have
 more vivid autumnal tints when grown in acid soils.

Ailanthis altissima (Tree of Heaven) D H25m (82ft) S15m (50ft).
 A fast-growing, eventually large tree with large leaves and clusters
 of cream flowers in mid-summer followed by scarlet winged fruits
 on female plants.

Arbutus unedo (Strawberry tree) E H4.5m (15ft) S4.5m (15ft). The
 only species of the genus to tolerate an alkaline soil, it has dark
 brown peeling bark. The strawberry-like fruits and white
 urn-shaped flowers appear at the same time in late summer.

Betula utilis var. *jacquemontii* (Kashmir birch) D H14m (45) S6m
 (20ft). The most striking of all the birches because of its smooth,
 dazzling white trunk and mature branches. The foliage turns a
 clear yellow in autumn.

Buddleja alternifolia D H3m (10ft) S3m (10ft). Smothered in clouds of pink/lilac flowers in June. Can be trained into a standard tree. Unlike the popularly grown Butterfly Bush (*B. davidii*), it flowers on the previous years' growth and is pruned back, if desired, immediately after flowering.

Cercidiphyllum japonicum (Katsura) D H15m (50ft) S12m (40ft). Lovely rounded leaves, bronze in spring turning a rich green and then yellow to purple in autumn. When the fallen leaves are crushed under foot they smell of burnt toffee or strawberry jam. Autumn tints are better on acid soils.

Cercis canadensis 'Forest pansy' D H7.5m (25ft) S7.5m (25ft). To my mind the most beautiful of all the trees with purple leaves. In spring, magenta buds open to pink flowers followed by red-purple, heart-shaped leaves.

Cornus alternifolia 'Argentea' D H7.5m (25ft) S7.5m (25ft). Layered habit with horizontal branches covered in small white-variegated leaves and white flowers in spring

Cornus controversa 'Variegata' (Wedding-cake tree) D H10m (30ft) S10m (30ft). Beautifully arranged, layered branches covered in bright green and creamy white leaves. Clusters of small, white flowers in summer.

Davidia involucrata (Pocket handkerchief tree; Dove tree) D H7.5m (25ft) S4.5m (15ft). It is a wonderful sight indeed when the handkerchief-like white bracts appear in May on trees 10 years old or more.

Eriobotrya japonica (Loquat) E H8m (26ft) S8m(25ft). Large exotic leaves and fragrant white flowers followed by pear-shaped orange-yellow fruits in warm summers. Surprisingly hardy. Requires some protection from cold winds.

Ginkgo biloba (Maidenhair tree) D H7.5m (25ft) S3m (10ft). The oldest known tree, dating back 200 million years. A conifer unlike any other with unmistakable rich green fan-shaped leaves which turn to a rich yellow before falling in autumn. Useful for its upright habit.

❃ OCTOBER

OCTOBER ❈

Juglans regia (Walnut) D 20 x 20m (60 x 60ft). Leaves starting
bronze-purple, turning to glossy green and edible nuts. The black
walnut (*Juglans nigra*), also with edible nuts, is a larger tree
H 30m (100ft) S22m (72ft).

Koelreuteria paniculata (Golden rain tree; Pride of India) D 10 x 10m
(30 x 30ft). Large sprays of yellow flowers in mid to late summer
are followed by bronze-pink, bladder-like fruits in hot summers.

Liriodendron chinense (Chinese tulip tree) D H25m (82ft) S12m
(40ft). Similar to the common tulip tree (L. tulipifera) but with a
faint russet blush to the uniquely characteristic leaves that look as
if they have been cut off flat at the base. Cup-shaped, orange-based,
greenish-white flowers appear in mid-summer on trees about ten
years old or more.

Magnolia wilsonii D 3.5 x 3.5m (12 x 12ft). The attraction of this
species is that its fragrant, cup-shaped, white flowers hang down
from the branch so that you can look up into them. Whereas most
magnolias prefer neutral to acid soils this species grows happily on
chalk.

Morus nigra (Black mulberry) D H6m (20ft) S10m (30ft). A tree
cherished for its serrated heart-shaped leaves, gnarled trunk and
delicious black fruits in late summer.

Parrotia persica (Persian ironwood) D H4.5m (15ft) S6m (20ft). Best
known for its brilliant autumnal tints and marbled, peeling bark.
Colours best in acid soils.

Picea breweriana (Brewer's weeping spruce) E H9m (30ft) S4m (13ft).
A beautiful conical conifer with graceful, weeping branches
bearing oblong purple cones.

Prunus lusitanica (Cherry laurel) E H6m (20ft) S10m (30ft). One
of the best of all the evergreen shrubs/small trees because of its
handsome shiny foliage. Responds well to shaping to a main trunk
and mushroom head.

Prunus subhirtella 'Autumnalis' (Winter cherry) D H4.5m (15ft) S3m
(10ft). An exceptional tree which can continue to produce
small white blossoms throughout the winter if it is a mild one.

Sorbus aria (Whitebeam) D H15m (50ft) S10m (30ft). Although the
white flowers in spring are nothing much to talk about, the silver-
grey leaves in spring which later turn to dark green and white-felted
beneath, make this one of the best foliage trees of all.

Sorbus 'Joseph Rock' D H10m (30ft) S7.5m (25ft). One of the best
trees for autumn colour. The leaves turn orange, red and purple in
beautiful contrast to the large clusters of yellow berries.

Stuartia pseudocamellia D H14m (46ft) S7.5m (25ft). White camellia-
like flowers appear in mid-summer. Ornamental, peeling bark.
Orange and red foliage tints in autumn. Acid soils only. Semi-shade.

Syringa 'Madame Lemoine' (Lilac) D H3.5m (12ft) S3m (10ft). One of
the most beautiful of all the lilacs, with panicles of white, scented
double flowers.

Trachycarpus fortunei (Chusan palm) E H9m (30ft) S2.5m (8ft). The
toughest of all the palms, hardy in many parts of the country.
Requires protection from cold winds especially when young.

The following trees should be avoided:

Picea abies (Christmas tree). However tempting it is to plant a small
rooted tree after the festivities, please resist the urge. This is a
forest plantation tree that eventually grows enormous, removing a
great deal of light from the garden.

Cupressocyparis leylandii (Leyland cypress). This is the most
contentious tree to have emerged in the last hundred years.
Irresistible as a very fast-growing, evergreen hedging plant, it has
caused more expensive law suits than any other plant in living
history. It should *only* be grown as a hedging plant in suburban
settings if the owner is prepared to keep it within bounds, at a
sensible height of 2m (6ft).

Rhus typhina (Stag's horn sumach). Ornamental though it is, with
large leaves that turn brilliant colours in early autumn, it sends
suckers for some distance even after the parent plant has died,
resulting in ruined lawns and choked shrubberies.

OCTOBER

OCTOBER TASKS

❈ Sow broad beans and sweet peas outside but keep cloches on hand to protect small plants from icy winds.

❈ Overgrown lilacs can have all older wood removed completely at ground level, leaving young shoots at the base. Regrowth from the base will be vigorous and after a couple of years all the new shoots should be cut back to ground level with the exception of the two or three strongest shoots which will eventually form the new tree.

❈ Plant wallflowers, forget-me-nots, winter-flowering pansies and primroses.

❈ Cut down asparagus once the foliage has turned yellow.

❈ Draw up soil around the base of brussels sprouts to prevent them from rocking about in strong winds. If they are grown in a very exposed spot they may have to be staked.

❈ Plant lavender in average (not enriched) soil, in a sunny position.

❈ Leave the vegetable plot rough-dug for the winter. The elements should succeed in breaking down the clods by spring.

❈ Cut Chinese Lanterns (*Physalis*) and dry them for winter flower arrangements.

❈ Lift dahlia tubers once the foliage has been blackened by frosts. Label them and store them in a dry, frost-free place for the winter.

❈ Rake leaves off the lawn regularly, otherwise they can damage turf.

❈ Cut out all remaining bunches of grapes otherwise they will rot, especially in colder temperatures.

❈ Loosen tree ties if they have begun to bite into the bark.

❈ Protect cauliflower curds from frosts by bending their leaves over them.

❈ Lift begonia tubers and gladioli corms, dry them off and store for the winter.

Planting for spring

NOVEMBER

I DID AFTER ALL DECIDE to leave every other one of the Leyland cypress stumps, so out of the original thirty-one 60ft trees, I now have sixteen 10ft poles. I was expecting the JCB to remove, deftly and effortlessly, the remaining 3ft stumps, rather like plucking pins out of a pincushion, but taking out the larger ones would have taken the freshly revealed, rotten rustic wooden fence with them, so I left them. This old fence is better than nothing although at some stage in the future it will need replacing.

I have swagged some ornamental rusty chain from the tops of the 10ft-tall poles on the south side of the big garden and it doesn't look half bad. The whole area has taken on a completely new feel now that my 40-mile view to the Lambourn Downs (via Didcot Power Station a mere 25 miles away) has been exposed. Near-to, it may be an eyesore but from this distance Didcot Power Station looks like a row of miniature thimbles. When the white smoke is lit by the evening sun you are rewarded with attractive orange wisps.

Can you imagine anyone wanting to block out such a glorious open country view in the first place? My neighbours are naturally delighted. One of them lives in a house called 'Long View', which would have contravened the Trades Descriptions Act if they had tried to sell it before I had cut down the trees. As I look out of my office window, which faces the garden, the bonfire is still active.

The result of burning the bulk of the thirty-one Leyland cypresses was an ash mountain 3ft high and 6ft across. Within its depths lurks hot ash and there is never any problem getting the fire going again of a cold and misty morn, even if it has rained all night. I also have a large woodpile which I intend leaving outside for two years to season. Phil, a countryman all his life, who cut down the trees and chopped up the remains, assures me that leylandii won't spit in the fire if seasoned well.

AN HISTORIC FIND?

Who would ever have guessed it? You hear of people finding unusual things in their gardens, the occasional historic artefact like a statue if they're lucky, but how often do people find an obsolete sewer? Well I have; behind the second line of Leyland cypress trees which I cut down was an inpenetrable jungle of brambles. Beyond a link-wire fence supported by concrete posts and the remains of wattle hurdles, I could just see a mass of triffid-like brambles with stems as thick as Havana cigars, monster nettles, scrubby elders and, dotted here and there, Hoover bags, broken bottles and assorted plastic detritus. As I fought my way through I suddenly came across a low brick wall. The pyromaniac came out in me and one match aimed at a thatch of dead nettles revealed a curving brick wall.

With feverish excitement, I lit a couple more Molotov cocktails and a round brick structure was revealed; then a large concrete chamber to one side; then a deep square-welled building on the other. Head-scratching didn't get me very far but a telephone call to the chairman of the village council did. I had exposed what had once been the sewer that serviced the school. My imagination has since run wild. Is this the heaven-sent answer to the swimming pool that my girls have been asking for? I can hear them now speaking to their friends over the telephone: 'If you aren't doing anything on Saturday, *do* come and swim in the sewer.'

Close behind the sewer at the very far end of the large garden in the corner, my land links up with the public footpath which sweeps along into open country. This means that I will be able to stroll through the garden when I take the dogs for a walk every morning, but what I do not want is uninvited guests coming in from the outside. I am not thinking particularly of the curious-minded, but rather of the sticky-fingered fraternity. Precautions can be taken in such vulnerable areas by planting shrubs with nasty spines (see page 118).

SCRAMBLED 'EGG'

The scrubby sycamores on the 'egg' off the green at the front of the house have gone, roots and all, thanks to four minutes' work by the JCB. One bite of its powerful jaws and that was that. With the help of Mark, a 26-year old ex-student of Art History, currently learning French, I have cut a 12ft-diameter circle where a scene of muddy carnage once stood. Mark lives bang next door and my three daughters have fallen madly in love with him. 'Oh Daddy! He has such beautiful eyes.' All I know is, he is reliable and punctual, works very hard and is a pleasant working companion, which is a rarity.

The circle has been planted with 2,000 common snowdrops (*Galanthus nivalis*). Spring bulbs always look best when planted in large drifts. Like anything else, there is an art to planting bulbs. I always find that little mixed groups say nothing to me at all.

In the centre of the circle I have planted a Hungarian Oak (*Quercus frainetto*), one of the fastest-growing species of the entire genus. It was the 60-year-old specimen at Anglesey Abbey in Cambridgeshire that opened my eyes to this particular species. Planted in 1932, it measures 55 feet high, with a spread of 50 feet, as I write.

Having recently planted a quercetum (a collection of oaks) for a client in Oxfordshire, I have got to know many of the species and varieties and so my choice was made all the easier. For my client I have planted nearly thirty different varieties and I felt very happy

NOVEMBER

about it until I learned that the arboretum at Batsford near Moreton-in-Marsh has nearly seventy. I see that my *RHS Plant Finder,* a book I refer to nearly every day (how on earth I survived without it before I cannot think), lists 152 species and varieties of oak. Such statistics are very humbling.

TREES ON THE SHOPPING LIST

I have added more trees to my shopping list, all chosen for very good reasons. First of all, two good trees for a country setting, the common walnut (*J. regia*) and a black mulberry (*Morus nigra*). I realize this last common name is not politically correct. In my *Plant Finder,* there are listed a couple of dwarf elders. Should we now call them Senior Citizens of Restricted Growth? What a nonsense it all is, but at least it makes us laugh. I would also like to include filberts and cobs, the smart cousins of the hazelnut.

Of the ornamental trees, I would have liked to include a Handkerchief tree (*Davidia involucrata*) for its hanky-like bracts and *Liriodendron chinense*, a rarer form of Tulip tree, for its leaves with a russet blush which look as if someone has come along and cut off their ends with a pair of scissors, but I fear I am too exposed for them up here. The village is 675ft above sea level and you have to pay for ravishing views with strong winds. I am hoping to succeed with the evergreen 'Killarney strawberry tree' (*Arbutus unedo*), with strawberry-like fruits and flowers which appear at the same time, in October. It is tolerant of my alkaline soil, unlike most species of *Arbutus.*

I also want to fit in a Maidenhair tree (*Ginkgo biloba*) and a Swamp cypress (*Taxodium distichum*) for their colourful displays in autumn; and a special birch, *Betula jacquemontii,* for its dazzling white bark – it is a tree which should always be planted where its bark reflects the setting sun. In the front I am going to plant an Evergreen oak, (*Quercus ilex*), flanked on either side by two ornamental shrubs, Persian ironwood (*Parrotia persica*) for its autumn colour and a particularly vigorous variety of Smoke tree, *Cotinus* 'Grace',

NOVEMBER

also for its dazzling autumn tints which look as if someone is shining a very powerful torch through huge, coin-shaped garnets.

I think the most exciting tree I have stumbled across in recent years is an ornamental form of Horsechestnut, *Aesculus* x *neglecta* 'Erythroblastos'. What makes this tree so special is that its emerging leaves in spring are a brilliant shrimp pink which later fades to pale green. About the only other tree to colour similarly in spring is the ubiquitously planted *Acer pseudoplatanus* 'Brilliantissimum', an ornamental form of the common sycamore. However, it is simply not in the same league – its leaves fade to a dull green for summer and it is so prone to disease and a wide range of physiological problems that I would not entertain it ever again.

✿ NOVEMBER

BUYING TREES

Before you buy a tree, it is worth doing some homework to find out how suitable it will be. Here are some of the major considerations:

❀ The most important thing is to find out how large it will eventually grow. The spread of its branches in maturity is as important as its height. You will soon see if your garden is big enough for a certain tree. (See page 40 for a selected list of garden trees.)

❀ Think what you want from your tree: spring blossoms? autumn tints? ornamental bark or leaves? Look them up in books and you may be able to find a tree that fulfils more than one of these criteria.

❀ For 'instant' effect, buy mature or semi-mature trees – but at a price. I believe in planting trees at around 60cm (2ft) high. The roots are then in proportion to the top growth and they get off to a better start.

❀ Evergreen or deciduous? Think twice before you choose an evergreen, especially in a small garden. It is far more difficult to grow plants underneath them because the ground around their base is deprived of light and rain.

NOVEMBER ❀

❀ When buying containerized trees, make sure they are not root-bound. In my experience this is seldom necessary, but if you are in doubt — perhaps the tree looks too large for its pot — have a look at the root system by tapping the plant out of its pot (ask someone to do this for you at the garden centre or nursery). If there is a lot of root growing round and round on itself, it means the tree has been in its container for too long. This can result in the roots continuing to grow in a spiral, resulting in poor growth. Trees, or any plant for that matter, with a lot of roots growing out of the bottom of their container should be avoided for the same reason.

Fastigiate trees

If you are limited for space and worried about depriving your garden of too much light, you can always choose a fastigiate species. These are trees that grow in a slender, upright shape. Many well-loved kinds of trees include a fastigiate form, such as:

Quercus robur 'Fastigiata' (Oak)
Fagus sylvatica 'Fastigiata' (Beech)
Ginkgo biloba 'Fastigiata' (Maidenhair tree)
Tulia platyphyllos 'Fastigiata' (Lime)

There also exist upright, single-stemmed fruit trees, such as a range of apples called 'Ballerina'; and a range of plums as well as apples called 'Minarette'.

PLANTING TREES

Containerized trees can be planted in full leaf so long as you disturb the roots as little as possible. Bare-rooted trees can only be planted during the dormant months, from November to mid-March. Evergreens are best planted in October and March. Trees get off to a good start if the soil they are planted in is well prepared.

PLANTING TREES

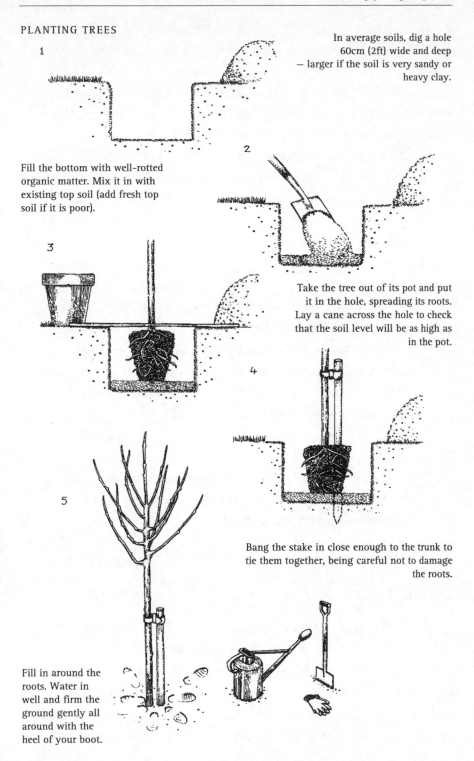

1

In average soils, dig a hole
60cm (2ft) wide and deep
— larger if the soil is very sandy or
heavy clay.

Fill the bottom with well-rotted
organic matter. Mix it in with
existing top soil (add fresh top
soil if it is poor).

3

2

Take the tree out of its pot and put
it in the hole, spreading its roots.
Lay a cane across the hole to check
that the soil level will be as high as
in the pot.

4

5

Bang the stake in close enough to the trunk to
tie them together, being careful not to damage
the roots.

Fill in around the
roots. Water in
well and firm the
ground gently all
around with the
heel of your boot.

NOVEMBER

COMMON MISTAKES

There are two common mistakes when it comes to planting trees:

✿ Planting too close to the house — this results in problems with root damage to foundations and underground pipes. To be really safe, this distance should not be less that 6m (20ft).

✿ Planting too close together. This means that the trees have to be thinned just as they are coming into their prime. As a general rule of thumb, keep to the same planting distance as above — 6m (20ft).

> TIPS: STAKING TREES
>
> ✿ Trials in recent years have proved that trees' trunks become stronger and thicken up quicker if supporting stakes are shorter rather than longer. As a rough guide, trees planted at six feet in height need only have a stake two feet high. The best ties look like small black belts. They are made of rubber and come with spacers so that the stake can be distanced from the tree if necessary. These ties are secured to the wooden stake with a nail to prevent it from slipping down and are easily loosened as the trunk expands.
>
> ✿ Never use wire to hold trees to their stakes. As the trunk expands, the wire digs into the wood resulting in poor growth and a very unhappy tree.

Felling trees

Always check whether you need permission from your local council before felling trees. To remove large trees, you will need to call in a tree surgeon, contracting him to remove the remaining stumps, if you want them cleared. Stumps can be a problem. You can keep them and make a feature out of them. For example:

✿ Mound a compost heap over the stump — this will help decompose it in the long run.

❀ If you're handy with a power saw, carve it into a seat (you need a stump of a minimum height of 1m (3ft) tall for this).

❀ Grow a climber such as clematis or honeysuckle over it. This makes an attractive, rural feature in a garden.

If you have no use for the stump, you must get rid of it to kill the roots and to stop new growth appearing at the base. Your alternatives are to remove it or to poison it. You can dig out a small stump by hand. A large stump requires a professional stump grinder – you can hire these, but try to share the costs with a neighbour, if you can, as they're not cheap. An efficient and safe way to poison stumps is to drill holes 2cm (1in) round and 5cm (2in) deep around the edge and half fill them with an ammonium sulphamate-based product. Then plug the holes or cover the whole stump with a water-proof shroud, securely tied.

TIP: EVERGREEN TRICK

 I succeeded in killing my Leyland cypresses by reducing each trunk to a pole. The majority of evergreen conifers will die if they are defoliated completely like this, but this is not the case with many other types of tree.

BEWARE HONEY FUNGUS

Stumps and roots left in the ground may encourage honey fungus. This is a killer fungus that spreads underground from the roots of one tree to another, for which there is no 100 per cent, guaranteed cure. As it is impossible to remove every trace of root when you remove a tree, there's always a remote possibility that this dreaded fungus may introduce itself in your garden.

The symptoms of honey fungus are neighbouring trees starting to die for no apparent reason – and you should contact a qualified tree surgeon immediately.

NATURALIZING SPRING BULBS

I underplanted my Hungarian oak with a large circle of 2,000 common snowdrops (*Galanthus nivalis*) so that when the tree matures, the shape of the canopy above will be mirrored by the snowdrops below.

'Naturalizing' means planting bulbs in positions where they will settle down and continue to flower perenially. Most spring bulbs will do this, with the exception of the majority of tulips. You may have noticed that when you plant fancy varieties, they are glorious in their first season but deteriorate in size and splendour thereafter until they stop flowering altogether. This is because tulips do not favour the soil conditions in Britain, or most other countries for that matter; they are not sufficiently well drained, nor dry enough in summer. Turkey is one country where they do flourish. However, our native tulip *Tulipa sylvestris*, normally with yellow flowers, does usually naturalize, as can the red-flowering *T. Couleur Cardinal* and a few others.

TIP: A LITTLE SCIENCE

❀ If green leaves are removed from a spring-flowering bulb before they have died down naturally, normally by the end of June, the bulbs are weakened for the following spring's display. This is easily explained. After a spring bulb has flowered, it recharges its batteries after its considerable exertions by re-energizing its bulb through photosynthesis. This is a word we all learned at school that describes the creation of energy by light coming into contact with chlorophyll in the green cells in plants. If green leaves are removed prematurely, the bulb's strength will be decreased, resulting in few if any flowers the following season.

❀ *Never* tie daffodil leaves in a knot after the flowers have faded. This reduces the amount of light getting to the leaves and hinders the process of photosynthesis.

Achieving the right look

The aim of naturalizing is to create a natural-looking drift, so never plant in straight lines or squares but in flowing shapes. The best place for a drift of bulbs is on the edge of a lawn, preferably around the base of trees. It always looks more effective if the same variety is planted in each swathe, rather than mixed. Small groups of bulbs dotted about on a lawn not only look messy and unnatural, but also interfere with mowing because the bulbs must be left to die down completely before the leaves are removed.

PLANTING BULBS

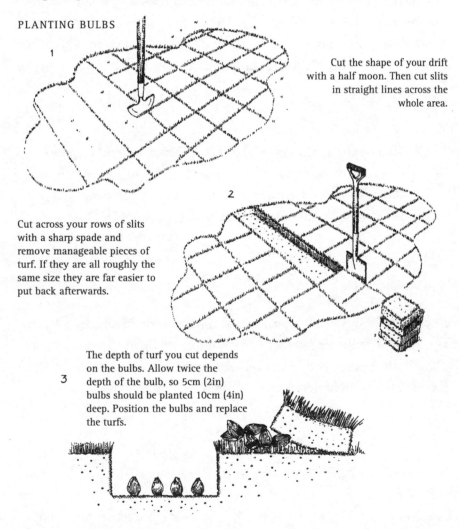

1

Cut the shape of your drift with a half moon. Then cut slits in straight lines across the whole area.

2

Cut across your rows of slits with a sharp spade and remove manageable pieces of turf. If they are all roughly the same size they are far easier to put back afterwards.

3 The depth of turf you cut depends on the bulbs. Allow twice the depth of the bulb, so 5cm (2in) bulbs should be planted 10cm (4in) deep. Position the bulbs and replace the turfs.

NOVEMBER

The best time to naturalize bulbs in a new lawn is before you seed or lay the lawn in September.

The easiest way to mark out the area for planting is with a hose pipe whose flexibility allows you to form rounds and curves. Once the bulbs are in, sow or turf over them.

Planting bulbs in an existing lawn can be quite a task – especially given that the ideal effect is of drifts, which means a lot of bulbs, even if not quite 2,000, as in my case.

Daffodils, snowdrops, crocuses, bluebells and winter aconites (*Eranthis hyemalis*) are ideal for planting in natural-looking swathes. The best display of snowdrops I have ever seen is at Painswick Rococo Gardens near Stroud in Gloucestershire. There are about two acres devoted entirely to them and it is a breath-taking sight in February.

 WARNING

There exist special bulb planters designed to remove plugs of earth for planting bulbs one at a time. They are of no use on stony ground, or where there are a lot of tree roots, because soil penetration is restricted.

Scattering bulbs

If you are planting a large area of daffodils or bluebells, you can scatter their bulbs like chicken feed and cover them where they land. These bulbs have special roots called 'contractile' roots, which readjust the bulb to the right depth and the right way up.

More ways to plant bulbs

Bulbs are also superb for spring colour in beds and borders but I feel they should only be planted under deciduous shrubs. Here they are unlikely to be disturbed when you dig in the border at any time of year and when they die down their messy dead leaves are hidden by the shrubs' foliage.

I do not think that snowdrops and winter aconites (*Eranthis hyemalis*), whose small, yellow, buttercup-like flowers sitting on pale green ruffles appear at the same time, look their best in containers. Mother Nature saw to it that in their natural habitat (they are native to many woodland areas in Europe) they appear in large drifts in, or on the edge of, deciduous woodland. I have grown to respect Mother Nature and her way of doing things.

The same basic rule applies to daffodils, crocuses, tulips, grape hyacinths and scillas, although for some unfathomable reason these do not look silly in pots and the more the merrier - all crammed together in a glorious cacophony of clashing hues, mixed with primroses and forget-me-nots for good measure. If you are very limited for space and can only garden in window boxes or pots, this mixed display of spring bulbs is exactly what you should aim for.

NOVEMBER

TIP: MOVING BULBS

If you have moved to a new garden and find that the snowdrops and winter aconites are growing in the wrong place, the best time to move them is immediately after flowering, before their leaves have completely died down, known as 'in the green'. The reason for this is because dry bulbs, sown in autumn, may have been overdried resulting in poor germination. In the case of all other spring bulbs you should only dig them up once the foliage has died back completely, store them in dry compost during the summer and plant them in their new permanent positions in early autumn.

Planting under trees

Growing plants under evergreens is tricky. If you remove their lower branches once they have reached about 6m (20ft) you can introduce plants, but the soil will have become very poor and powder dry and will need replacing.

Deciduous trees are altogether easier when it comes to planting underneath them, mainly because the ground around their base receives dappled light in summer and plenty of moisture in winter. However, not all plants like growing beneath deciduous trees because they do not like being dripped on.

Here is a selection of plants for growing underneath trees:

E = Evergreen S/E = Semi-Evergreen H = Height S = Spread

Brunnera macrophylla (Siberian bugloss) H45cm (18in) S60cm (24in). Small, star-shaped, forget-me-not like flowers in early spring. Good ground cover.

Cornus canadensis (Creeping dogwood) H10-15cm (4-6in), S30cm (12in) or more. White bracts in late spring and early summer followed by red berries.

Dicentra spectabilis (Bleeding heart, Dutchman's trousers) H75cm (30in) S50cm (20in). Heart-shaped, pinkish-red and white flowers in spring.

Fargesia murieliae (previously named *Arundinaria murieliae*; also called *Thamnocalamus spathaceus*) (Bamboo) E H up to 3.5m (11ft 6in). Graceful arching canes and masses of small leaves. A spreader.

Geranium macrorrhizum (Cranesbill) H38cm (15in) S60cm (24in). Excellent ground cover with magenta flowers in early summer. The cranesbills are many and varied.

Helleborus niger (Hellebore; Christmas rose; Lenten rose) E 45 x 45cm (18 x 18in). Woodland plant with cup-shaped, white flowers and golden stamens in winter and spring.

Hosta undulata var. *albomarginata* (also called *H.* 'Thomas Hogg'), (Funkia, Plantain lily), H45cm (1ft 6in), S60cm (2ft). Trumpet-shaped, pale mauve flowers in summer and green, pale cream and

One of my favourite vegetables – everlasting spinach – under the spider gate.

ABOVE The silver and white border with splashes of yellow is coming on a treat.

LEFT Geranium 'Ann Folkard' with magenta flowers and a hint of yellow on the leaf, clambering over potted hostas.

RIGHT All gardens should contain a dovecote – they are such attractive objects.

BELOW My collection of hand-turned terracotta flower pots with tomatoes, peppers, sieves and my favourite watering can as companions.

LEFT A lewesia –
perfectly suited to a
small hole in a
stone wall.

BELOW A close-up
of the silver, yellow
and white border: a
cool and calming
mixture.

white leaves. Just one of hundreds of hostas widely sold.

Lamium maculatum (Dead nettle) S/E H15cm (6in) S1m (3ft). Good ground cover plant with mauve-tinged leaves with a central silvery stripe and mauve-pink flowers in mid-spring.

Luzula sylvatica 'Marginata' (Greater woodrush) E H30cm (12in) S indefinite. An ornamental grass with green leaves with white margins and brown flower spikes in summer.

Pieris japonica E H3m (10ft), S7m (23ft). Glossy, dark green foliage and dark flowers in spring. For acid soils only.

Pleioblastus aurocomus (used to be called *Arundinaria viridistriata*) (Bamboo) E H1.5m (4ft 6in). A spreader.

Pseudosasa japonica (used to be called *Arundinaria japonica)* (Bamboo) E up to 5m (15ft) tall with broad leaves 35cm (14in) long. A spreader.

Pulmonaria angustifolia (Lungwort) H23cm (9in) S20-30cm (8-12in). Narrow leaves and pink-tinged, dark blue flowers.

Rhododendron yakushimanum E H1m (3ft) S1.5m (5ft). A neat species of compact habit with pink flowers that fade to near white in late spring. For acid soils only.

Symphytum grandiflorum (Comfrey) H25cm (10in) S60cm (24in). Lance-shaped, hairy leaves and creamy flowers in spring. Good ground cover.

Tellima grandiflora (Fringecups) S/E 60 x 60cm (24 x 24in). Heart-shaped, hairy leaves and small, bell-shaped, creamy flowers in late spring.

Tiarella cordifolia (Foamflower) E H15-20cm (6-8in) S30cm (12in) or more. Lobed, pale green leaves and profuse white flowers in late spring and early summer.

NOVEMBER TASKS

❈ Plant tulip bulbs.

❈ Lag outdoor taps if they are not to burst after freezing bouts of weather.

❁ Continue to plant fruit trees and bushes and deciduous trees.

❁ Parsley should be protected with cloches to protect it from cold weather.

❁ Where hardy agapanthus is grown in containers, bubble wrap should be secured round the pots to prevent the roots from being damaged by penetrating frosts.

❁ The greenhouse can be lined with bubble wrap to conserve heat.

❁ Large clumps of Michaelmas daisies can be divided once the flowers have faded.

❁ Winter greens may have to be netted against hungry birds.

❁ Turf can be laid anytime during the winter so long as the ground is neither waterlogged nor frozen.

❁ Drain hose pipes and put them away for the winter.

❁ Grow mustard and cress on a sunny window sill in a warm room.

❁ Burn all rose leaves infected by black spot. If left on the plant or even on the ground this fungal disease can easily overwinter.

Winter dreams

DECEMBER

EUREKA! AT LAST I HAVE FOUND A BOWL. As I dig I find pieces of old clay pipe (the smoking variety), usually about 2.5cm (1in) long and I am collecting them in a bucket. My aim is to arrange them as a collage behind glass, just as they have done at Sudeley Castle which I visited this summer; whether or not I ever get around to it is another matter. My house used to be a pub, so I expect to find plenty more.

Someone explained to me the other day why it is that I keep on finding so many pieces of old clay pipes. Apparently in olden days, long white clay pipes could be hired from the landlord and then filled with tobacco from a jar for a penny or whatever a fill. The same pipe was smoked by a succession of people who each snapped off the end for the next person, for reasons of hygiene. In old pictures you always see smart gentlemen smoking long, pristine pipes and the yokels short, stubby ones. Presumably they became cheaper the shorter they became. Women used to smoke a lot in those days as well – the bowl in the shape of a shoe that I have found must have been made with a woman in mind? They used to make clay pipes in the village but stopped some time during the nineteenth century – the last remaining man to make them having gloried in the nickname 'Old Gooseberry'.

THE BEGINNINGS OF THE BORDER

The silver and white border — anyway the planning of it — is coming on and I have now decided to allow the occasional glimpse of pale yellow. How can I not include the queen of the white Japanese anemones, *A* x *hybrida* 'Honorine Jobert', with white flowers centred with such showy yellow stamens, that last for three months in late summer and into autumn? I have also added a prized shrub, an ornamental elder, *Sambucus racemosa* 'Tenuifolia', which up until now has lived in a large pot and was starting to resent it. This beauty looks exactly like *Acer palmatum,* var. *dissectum,* unless you study it at very close quarters, and in early spring is covered in pale yellow fluffy balls the size of large marbles.

Silver-leaved santolinas are perfect for this border and I must have 'Edward Bowles', with his delightful creamy-white small flowers. *Santolina virens*, although I love it, would be too brash, the flowers of too strong a yellow like so many of its cousins. Thanks to the last owner of this house, a Dr Bartlett who was both a priest and a dentist, I have a 6ft-tall magnolia (nothing out of the ordinary, *M.* x *soulangiana*, I think). It was this tree that triggered off the idea of a silver and white border because it constituted an already existing white display and I couldn't think of a better colour than silver to go with it. I have already planted one of my favourite of all the herbaceous perennials, the white-flowering willowherb (*Epilobium angustifolium album*) which rampages but does not self-seed like its common pink-flowering, waste ground-loving cousin. The plant list for this border doesn't by any means end here.

THE JCB STORY

The excavating machine, the JCB, is named after its inventor Joseph Cyril Bamford CBE, who now lives in Switzerland. The story goes that he has never looked back after putting a front loader onto his tractor on his farm in Staffordshire back in the '50s. He and later his son

Anthony (now Sir Anthony) continued to perfect the machine to the one we know today. The JCB has been such a success that the family has grown enormously rich as a result. I cannot think of any other family to have amassed such a fortune through a single machine. Mr Rolls and Mr Royce certainly did not. I love hearing success stories.

Anyway, that is neither here nor there. The point is, I have had the JCB back, with its massive driver Tim, whose girlfriend, I have since discovered, is a boxer. Despite his somewhat awesome bulk, Tim is a gentle fellow with a lovely sense of humour. When I asked him how much a JCB weighed, he said, grinning, 'Eight and a half ton. Not much really, although I wouldn't like one to land on my head.' The most satisfying part of the day was watching the old cesspit disappear out of my life for ever. I did at one stage have ideas of turning it into a pond but it has proved far easier to fill it in. Whereas before the garden was a sea of dead grass, it is now a sea of mud.

A ROUND POND AND STRAIGHT LINES

I have scooped out the round pond in a dish-shape to a depth of about 2ft in the centre and 10ft in diameter and lined it with a flexible liner, having first lined the crater with an inch of builder's sand. The most important thing to remember when laying down a flexible liner for a pond is to make sure you get rid of all organic matter first. If you do not, methane gas forms under the liner and lifts it up, making it look as if you have got a semi-submerged hippo in your pond. I remember this happening at the first of the International Garden Festivals in Liverpool; people were running around frantically trying to tread out the air bubbles in a large pond just before HM the Queen arrived.

My pond is round, as will be the hedge surrounding it. The circle somehow wins hands down over all the other geometric shapes. I do not rule out any other shape for ponds, with the exception of kidney-shapes as I see little point in being constantly reminded of one's innards. Square ponds have their place but I always try to avoid

❧ DECEMBER

angular shapes in gardens. Capability Brown once said 'Nature abhors straight lines.' He certainly had a point but that does not mean that gardens should necessarily be devoid of them. After all, what could be more glorious than the long straight avenue of Wellingtonias at Stratfield Saye or the Long Water at Hampton Court Palace? I think that Brown should be considered a more controversial figure whose halo should not be allowed to shine quite so brightly. After all, he did destroy umpteen formal walled gardens in his obsession to create 'romantic landscapes' and therefore one can justifiably argue that he was just as much a vandal as a genius. He was shrewd (you can tell he was sharp by looking at his portrait which hangs at Wilton House in Wiltshire) and realized a good thing when he saw it, jumping onto the William Kent bandwagon as he did.

The story of how the Classical Landscape Movement came into being is a fascinating one and involves many of the greatest names in literature and the arts. It was sparked off by seventeenth-century Rome-based artists like Claude Lorraine, Nicholas Poussin and Salvator Rosa who painted classically inspired pictures based on stories written by the likes of Ovid, Horace and especially Pliny whose writings and descriptions of his own villa were the only extensive records to survive the Augustan period (about AD1)

Many of these pictures represented an idyll of ancient Rome, with classical buildings enhancing lush landscapes. They greatly inspired the rich patrons of the day who went to great lengths to emulate them. William Kent and Charles Bridgeman were the landscape architects to lay out such grandiose schemes. 'Capability' (Lancelot) Brown followed close behind.

If there was ever an unsung hero of this movement it is Henry Hoare, an amateur gardener belonging to the banking family who started to create those wonderful gardens at his house at Stourhead in 1741, the very same year that Lancelot Brown landed his first job as head gardener at Stowe in Buckinghamshire.

It is 6 December and England is being swept by viciously cold winds from the Balkans bringing snow with them. The ground is unworkable but at least my sea of mud looks prettier, as if a huge chocolate cake has been sprinkled with dry icing sugar.

HIRING AN EARTH-MOVING MACHINE

I talked about how quickly and efficiently the JCB helped with the building of my garden. Not all gardens need turning around as much as mine and therefore you may not need to use earth-moving machinery at all, but I did need one to trench for hedging and pipes, level various areas, break up old cesspits and for many other jobs. One particular job, the removal of the sycamores from the front of the house, that proved the JCB's worth. It took 48 seconds to uproot them. Based on a JCB costing £100 for an eight-hour day to hire, this operation cost me about 21 pence. When you compare this to a good labourer (several pounds per hour), who could not have done it in less than two hours (including the removal of the roots), the financial benefits are obvious if you need such a machine for a whole day.

PLANNING A BORDER

Planning a border, or a whole garden for that matter, is in many ways like painting a picture, except that the paint continues to move on the canvas. My silver and white border, I know, will change every year. It is a moveable feast and a very delicious one. Once I had decided on a silver and white border I made a list of plants I wanted to include from various books, although I had already made a mental list right from the start. Collecting the plants was the greatest fun, making list after list, followed by deletions and additions, a job I relished on cold winter evenings when I closed my eyes and dreamed.

You may have an existing plant, like my magnolia, that inspires you to a colour scheme or theme for a border. If not, look at borders in gardens and books. Decide on a scheme that appeals to you. Some ideas are:

❦ DECEMBER

❋ A cool blue and white border

❋ A hot red, yellow and orange border

❋ A distinct colour scheme, such as mine: silver and white or yellow
and blue or pink and mauve, for example

❋ A hectic, multicoloured border

To help make up your mind about the border, look at its situation:

❋ How much sun will it get?

❋ Is it shaded by trees?

❋ What kind of soil does it have?

❋ Its position — along a wall or lining a path?

A cool combination of woodland plants would look better under
trees, but a sunny border would look wonderful in vibrant colours.
My border gets plenty of sun, so obvious choices were plants with
small, plump, often hairy silvery leaves which excel in open sunny
sites. These include the santolinas (cotton lavenders), artemesias
(wormwoods), stachys (lamb's ears) and verbascums.

Contrast for variety

In any border it is important to juxtapose plants with varying shape
and leaf texture so that they contrast with each other, a guarantee for
happy neighbours. For example, sword-like iris leaves look splendid
alongside a clipped box ball; the lush leaves of a hosta look excellent
alongside the woolly foliage of santolina; and the tall silvery stem
and leaves of *Onopordum acanthium* make a good contrast with the
dark green leaves of the neat, mound-shaped *Cistus corbariensis*.

Structure

It is important in any border to plant low-growing plants at the front
and tall at the back. Some tall plants are slow-growing and will

therefore not be very tall when they start off. While you allow them time to grow you can plant some fast-growing plants for almost instant height.

My fast growers are Arundo donax (Giant reed), an ornamental perennial grass which can grow as high as 6m (20ft) in one season (although I doubt it will attain that height at this altitude – over 700ft) and Onopordum acanthium to grow to at least 3m (10ft). My slow growers include magnolia and white lilac.

Most of the herbaceous plants are towards the centre of the borders and cushion plants like *Cerastium tomentosum* (Snow in summer), *Geranium sanguineum* 'Album' and the white horned violet (*Viola cornuta Alba*) towards the front.

I found it important to group several plants together in twos and threes so that they grew into one large clump. Some plants, such as the white horned violet, will obligingly seed themselves some distance from the original plants, giving rise to a pleasant patchwork of clumps of flowers of the same kind repeating throughout the border.

During the first season a border looks very bare. In my silver and white border, in order to help fill up the larger gaps, I planted *Nicotiana sylvestris*, a flowering tobacco with a mass of trumpet-shaped white flowers clustered on the top of tall stems and *Senecio cineraria* 'Silver Dust', with lacy leaves that are so silver that they appear almost white.

Extending the season

It was very important to plan this border so that there was always something to look at and admire during the whole year.

A good plant for winter decoration is variegated stinking iris (*Iris foetidissima* 'Variegata'), also the Chusan palm (*Trachycarpus fortunei*), one of the toughest of all the palms, which I have tucked into a corner where it gets protection from icy winter winds. Late

❖ DECEMBER

summer can be a tricky time of year when it comes to having enough plants on show. Apart from *Anemone* x *hybrida* 'Honorine Jobert', I also included *Aster novae-angliae* 'Herbstschnee' ('Autumn snow') and white cactus dahlias for the same reason.

Making mistakes

Everyone makes mistakes. I planted *Artemesia* 'Powis Castle' too far towards the front of the border and, because it grew too large too quickly, I later had to move it further back. I made exactly the same mistake with my variegated honesty (*Lunaria annua* 'Alba Variegata'). Making mistakes is the only practical way to learn about happy planting combinations. Sometimes things you do by accident happen to look wonderful; if they do not, you can move them and try again. This is part of the joy of making a border. It is always changing and never 'finished'.

SUMMARY OF BORDER DESIGN

✿ Consider the site of the border.

✿ Decide on a colour or theme.

✿ Plan the structure - tall at the back, small at the front.

✿ Aim for variety

Plants in my silver and white (with a hint of yellow) border. (Unless otherwise stated these are herbaceous perennials.)

SH = Shrub C = Climber T = Tree A = Annual B = Biennial

Artemesia 'Powis Castle' SH. Deservedly popular as it does not
   collapse in a mess like so many other species and varieties of

artemesia. It can be cut back hard every spring.

Arundo donax. Tall ornamental grass, excellent for the back of a
border.

Aster novae-angliae 'Herbstschnee' (also called *A. n-a.* 'Autumn
snow'). A beautiful New England aster with tall white flowers in
late summer.

Bergenia 'Beethoven'. A beautiful variety of Elephant's
Ears with pure white flowers in spring. It makes a nice change
from all those ubiquitously planted pink-flowering varieties.
B. 'Silberlicht' (*B.* 'Silver Light') also has white flowers.

Cistus corbariensis (Rock rose) SH. A dense and neat shrub with
white flowers with a yellow centre in late spring and early
summer.

Cynara cardunculus (Cardoon). Chosen for its elegant, deeply cut,
silver leaves 90cm-1.2m (3-4ft) long and delicious flower heads,
needs plenty of space and is not to be confused with the Globe
artichoke (*C. scolymus*) whose leaves are not so ornamental and
whose flower heads are not as prickly.

Convallaria majalis 'Albostriata' (Variegated lily-of-the-valley). This
is one of my favourite plants of all. With scented flowers identical
to the common lily-of-the-valley, the leaves are narrowly striped
in creamy yellow.

Convolvulus cneorum SH. A silvery-leaved small shrub, not fully
hardy, with white bindweed-like flowers. It is best grown in a pot
buried in the soil so that it can easily be taken into the greenhouse
for the winter.

Digitalis purpurea f. albiflora (White foxglove). Although strictly
classified as biennials, foxgloves can be encouraged to perennate
if the flowers are cut back down to the ground the minute they
fade. (The same applies to hollyhocks.)

Geranium sanguineum 'Album'. A favourite cranesbill of mine, of
neat and compact habit, hummock-forming, which can grow as
high as 60cm (2ft).

Hemerocallis 'Joan Senior'. I think this is an exceptional day lily. It

❧ DECEMBER

has off-white flowers and yellowish-green throat.

Lunaria annua 'Alba Variegata' (Variegated honesty) B. So much
more exciting than the bog standard ordinary purple honesty, with
white flowers and leaves generously edged in white. A biennial
that self-seeds very obligingly, but do not grow it close to its
common purple cousin otherwise it will not come true.

Onopordum acanthium (Cotton thistle, Scotch thistle) B. A tall-
growing (up to 3m/10ft) thistle-like plant with spiny-toothed,
grey-green leaves and small pale purple or white flower-heads.
(If the flowers prove pale purple I shall turn a blind eye.) An
architectural biennial for the back of the border.

Paeonia mlokosewitschii (Peony). Despite the fact that its specific
name is totally impossible to pronounce, it represents the boldest
splash of yellow in this border with its cool lemon-yellow, single
flowers in May. One of this plant's strengths is that its foliage
remains decorative throughout the summer, which is more than
you can say for practically every other herbaceous peony.

Philadelphus 'Beauclerk' (Mock orange) SH. Large, single,
cup-shaped, white scented flowers in summer.

Phlox paniculata 'Blue Ice'. I have always grown phlox because their
appearance in late summer is so welcome and they are so robust.

Rosa 'Sombreuil' C. White, fully double, sweetly scented flowers.
And *R*. 'Boule de Neige' SH. A Bourbon shrub rose with an upright
habit; has fully double white flowers with a strong scent.

Stachys byzantina (also called *S. lanata* and *S. olympica*; Lamb's
Ears). An indispensable carpeter with soft, woolly, grey leaves that
remind me of my childhood. I cut off the magenta flowers before
they open not only because they spoil the silver and white effect,
but also because they tend to flop and spoil the carpet effect.

Syringa 'Madame Lemoine' (Lilac) T. For her large, double, white,
scented flowers from creamy buds in May.

Viola cornuta (Horned violet). A small, cushion-forming perennial
pansy ideal for the front of a border. If they are clipped back hard
in July, a second flush of flowers will appear in August and

September. Buy these plants when in flower as they come in either pale violet or white.

AN OBSERVATION

The reason why foxglove plants live longer if their flowers are cut immediately after they have flowered is because they are deprived of being able to produce ripened seed and therefore remain alive in the hope that they will be able to do just that the following season. The same applies to many roses, which is why we are encouraged to dead-head. With roses, this often results in a second flush of flowers in the same season, hence the description 'remontant'.

TIP: EDIBLE FLOWERS

The watery, slightly sugary flowers of day lilies make exciting, colourful additions to salads (along with those of nasturtium).

RAISED BEDS

Raised beds are especially useful for elderly or disabled gardeners as both can garden at eye-level from a wheelchair or in a kneeling position. However, they can be included in any garden for growing a whole variety of plants to give 'instant height'. They are ideally suited for growing alpines or, indeed, vegetables, as the soil inside them warms up that bit earlier in spring when the warmth of the sun penetrates their sides. (Strictly speaking, an alpine is a plant that is adapted to growing above the tree line on a mountain. However, we use the term to describe plants that look good in raised beds, rock gardens and miniature gardens.)

The ideal raised bed, aesthetically, is of old stone laid dry, with several plants like *Alchemilla mollis*, *lewesias* and *Erigeron karvinskianus* growing between the cracks. If you are planning to build one in brick, especially new brick, it is important to leave gaps in the brickwork for such plants in order to interrupt the stark boxiness of the construction. Alternatively, small (10cm/4in) terracotta flower pots can be inserted in the gaps in vertical surfaces of raised beds, slightly turned upwards so that the compost is less likely to be leached away by heavy rain. (For more information on plants in walls, see pages 87-89.) Attractive old bricks are, of course, more expensive, as they are in shorter supply these days owing to the fact that there is less demolition of older properties taking place. During the two or three decades following World War II, they were easy to find and reasonably priced. Cement blocks, peat blocks, treated wooden planks, floorboards or marine plywood, vertical pavers or wooden railway sleepers are other alternatives – but be warned: on hot days wooden railway sleepers become sticky with and smell strongly of tar.

In new walls grow plants in small terracotta pots inserted between the bricks.

Building a raised bed using marine plywood

The advantage of building a free-standing raised bed in wood with strengthened corners is that it does not require a foundation, unlike stone, brick and other heavier materials. A good height and depth for a raised bed is about 1m (3ft), to allow easy access to plants. Marine plywood is an attractive (and comparatively cheap) material to use for raised beds, using 2.5cm (1in) thick sheets, supported on every corner with 8cm (3in) square posts. Before filling with stone and compost, the wood must be treated with a bitumastic paint to delay the rotting process on the inside of the bed where the wood is in contact with the damp soil.

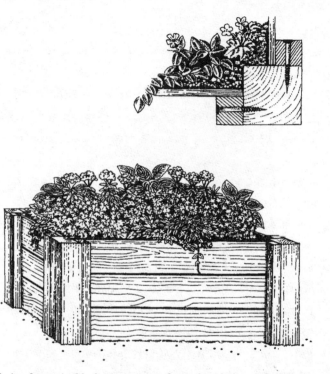

A simple design for a raised bed using marine plywood, with the reinforced corner construction shown above.

Wooden raised beds are most likely to decay at the base and therefore it is vital first to put in a drainage layer of stone or crocks so that excess water can escape easily. 'Weep' holes, small sections of plumber's pipe inserted through the wood, can also be added to help drainage. A layer of well-rotted organic matter is then placed over the drainage material at the bottom and the rest filled in with compost. After planting, mulch the soil to reduce water evaporation.

The soil in raised beds tends to dry out faster than soil in the ground. You may compensate for this by watering it with an automatic watering system, or by installing a tap nearby.

ROCKERIES

Before you decide on building a rockery, consider the following:

❀ Make sure you have the space for a rockery and choose the position with care, otherwise you will end up with an incongruous mess. A corner of a garden can prove to be a good place.

❀ A rockery must look like a natural rock formation, not just a pile of stones. Properly built rockeries using large stones and boulders are expensive. This is often due to haulage costs, apart from the cost of the stone itself.

❀ There exists a large variety of different stone, ranging enormously in both hue and shape. The best way to choose the right sort of rock for your garden is to visit a specialist supplier so that you can compare one with another. Very often your local stone fits into the landscape better, especially if your house is built of it.

❀ Try to incorporate a natural-looking stream running through the rockery, with the addition of a pond close to it in which an electric submersible pump can be positioned.

❀ Always get a rockery built by specialists unless you are 100 per cent confident that you can do the job yourself.

❀ Rockeries are high maintenance. Do you have the time to keep it clear of weeds?

MINIATURE GARDENS

Growing alpines in the miniature landscape provided by a stone sink can be fascinating. To disguise a glazed sink to look like stone, make up a mixture of two parts sifted moss peat, one part silver sand and one part cement. Moisten the dry mixture and then paint the clean glazed surface with PVA adhesive and apply the mixture by hand. Leave the surface fairly rough and uneven. Cover the sink with polythene and leave it to dry for about three weeks.

If you do not have a china (or stone) sink to convert into a trough garden for alpines, there is a way of making your own stone lookalike trough.

❀ Choose two strong cardboard boxes, so that one sits inside the other with an 8-10cm (3-4in) gap between them.

❀ Mix equal parts of sharp sand, cement and moss-peat substitute.

❀ First put an even layer of the mixture into the bottom of the large box and insert a wooden peg or small section of pipe in the centre to act as a draining hole.

❀ Fill in around the edge between the two boxes with your fake stone mixture. Leave for four days before removing the mould and drainage pipe.

❀ The smooth finish should be distressed to give it a rough, natural-looking surface either with a chisel or by having more of the mixture daubed onto it.

When positioning your sink or trough, make sure it is level and put it in an open, sunny site. For good drainage, mix sharp grit into the compost when filling the sink and arrange a few interesting stones or shells on the surface. After planting, cover the surface with sharp grit or gravel to conserve water.

Here is a selection of plants for the miniature garden:

Aquilegia saximontana. Blue-green leaves and short-stemmed blue
   and white flowers in spring.
Carex firma 'Variegata'. A tiny sedge with stiff leaves edged in cream.
Dianthus alpinus 'Joan's Blood'. A neat plant with crowded bronze
   leaves and blood-red flowers in early summer.

❀ DECEMBER

Draba bryoides. A dense mat of emerald-green with small yellow flowers in spring.

Gentiana verna angulosa. Deep blue flowers with a white eye. Stunning during late spring.

Potentilla eriocarpa. A mat of grey-green leaves. Flowers throughout the summer and autumn.

Saxifraga carniolica. Silver-grey, tightly packed leaves with 'beading' along the edges. Creamy flowers in early spring.

Saxifraga 'Maria Luisa'. Beautiful silver-grey rosettes and pure white flowers in December and January.

Silene keiskei var. *minor.* A campion-like herbaceous plant with deep pink flowers in late summer.

Teucrium aroanium. Grey leaves and hooded pale purple flowers in summer.

Thalictrum kiusianum. Graceful fern-like leaves and fuzzy purple flowers in spring.

Wahlenbergia pumilio. Grey-green tufts with upturned funnel-shaped flowers in varying shades of blue in summer.

DECEMBER TASKS

❀ Remove flower heads on tender geraniums under glass. They should not be allowed to be at all energetic at this time of year.

❀ Young conifers should be protected from cold winds with a hessian shroud.

❀ Cut conifer sprigs and holly and gather fir cones for Christmas decoration.

❀ Water houseplants sparingly. Overwatering houseplants accounts for most fatalities.

❀ Check stored fruit for any signs of mouse attack or rotting. Discard all those affected.

❀ Rhubarb can start to be forced under the staging of a heated greenhouse.

❀ Firm around the base of young plants lifted by the frost.

❀ Prolong the flowering season of tender cyclamen by keeping them in the cool, out of direct sunlight and only watering when the leaves start to droop.

❀ Cut back self-clinging climbers like Ivy and Virginia Creeper to within a couple of feet of gutter height.

❀ Leave parsnips in the gound for harvesting when they are needed.

❀ Plant bare-rooted roses in enriched ground. All bare-rooted plants can be heeled in somewhere temporarily until such time as their permanent positions are ready for them.

❀ Fill a vase with forsythia, horsechestnut, flowering currant or witch hazel for winter decoration.

DECEMBER

A really good start

JANUARY

I SPENT THE FIRST FIVE YEARS OF MY LIFE in an old manor
house between Abergavenny and Raglan, in Monmouthshire. On
the stone roof tiles above the kitchen door, a great cushion of
houseleeks grew and I have fond memories of the welcoming kitchen
and Nanny's fudge in the big old fridge behind the door.

My father sold the house in the early 1950s and my aunt and her
husband eventually bought it. When the roof was replaced in the late
1980s, my cousin William Prichard thoughtfully transplanted the
same houseleeks into a border by the croquet lawn. (William was
British Open Croquet Champion in 1980 and the site of his croquet
lawn was previously a riding school where my father trained
Foxhunter – together they won a Gold Medal at the Helsinki Olympic
Games in 1952.)

Anyway, a year ago my cousin gave me a piece of that original
houseleek which has now become the most important plant in my
garden, for sentimental reasons. I have planted it in the wall in the
front of the house in one of the special planting gaps I had built
between the stones. Every time I look at that plant I can taste
Nanny's fudge.

I have been very selective of plants for this wall and have included *Valerian phu* 'Aurea' for its yellow young foliage and white flowers

smaller than than those of *V. officinalis*. Valerian is such a rewarding plant as its white, red or pink flowers appear intermittently from spring to autumn if they are cut back immediately after fading and they grow so obligingly in the meanest crack in paving or wall. I will later include *Erigeron karvinskianus* and on the shaded side of the wall I plan to introduce *Lewisia cotyledon*. It is these little touches to a garden, 'fine tuning' as a friend calls them, that win the day.

THE HOLLYHOCK HEDGE

On the sunny side of this wall I have planted a hollyhock hedge, with twenty plants spaced just under 60cm (2ft) apart, to give me plenty of colour from June to September. I bought my hollyhock plants by mail order and I gave them royal treatment, with soil enriched with well-rotted manure down to 45cm (18in) and one Osmocote capsule at the very bottom of each hole. I use Osmocote capsules with every planting. They release nutrients below ground when plants most need them – when the soil is warm and damp – and shut up shop when the ground is wet and chilly.

EXTERIOR DECOR

The principles of exterior decoration are similar to those of interior. A mirror makes all the difference to an otherwise unprepossessing out-door or indoor wall, colour combinations in bedrooms and reception rooms as well as herbaceous borders are all the rage at the moment and lighting can make all the difference to the ambience of a room whether it be outside or in. I am thinking of lamps in particular and the shape of their stems and shades (I have never been one for over-head lights). I have been looking for waterproof lamps for outdoor use and have at last come across a source. Made of brass with a verdigris finish, they have slim stems and simple cone shades. They come with stems decorated in ivy leaves, ears of wheat or lotus leaves. I have chosen ivy leaves but I may remove them later.

FINDING A FENCE

The north-facing boundary of the large garden is overlooked by several houses. While I am on good terms with all my neighbours, I do not particularly like looking at their washing drying so I must have a boundary fence. Looking through all my catalogues, I came to the conclusion that, out of all the fencing there is available, there is little to beat the aesthetic qualities of wattle fencing hurdles. Their hand-woven appeal scores high in my book against the ubiquitous overlap alternatives.

Fate was on my side. One morning I received by post a large brown envelope and inside it were details of products supplied by a local timber firm. There it was staring me in the face – the 6 x 6ft wattle fencing I was looking for, made in hazel. What is also appealing about these hurdles is that they are 100 per cent environmentally friendly. Further, they are made in the most traditional, old-fashioned way.

There is a group of men, many of whom have left professional careers and opted for a simpler, quieter life, who now live in caravans in the depths of the New Forest for most of the year. They devote their time to hand-weaving hazel arches, seats and hurdles, using twigs from ancient coppices. A man can only make six hurdles a week, so mass production for DIY sheds and their like is quite out of the question and this I find appealing.

WELCOME THE COLD WEATHER

The weather over Christmas and New Year was appalling. At one stage it froze hard after a wet shower, resulting in even gravel drives becoming ice rinks. I tried to take the dogs for a walk but had to give up as I couldn't even cross the narrow lane by the house. We only *just* missed having a white Christmas much to the chagrin of grown-ups and children alike.

The garden couldn't be looking more dead, but we gardeners

❁ JANUARY

should always be grateful for cold winter spells. Not only are harmful insect populations reduced but also it helps to break up ground that has been left rough-dug.

A GOOD START IN LIFE

After many years of gardening, I have learned that the most important thing you can do is give a plant the best possible start to life – just like babies. The more tender loving care (including a good diet) you give to plants and babies when they're young, the better the chance that they will grow up into decent, healthy plants and human beings. This applies particularly to trees, shrubs and herbaceous perennials, which will be in the same spot for many years.

For planting trees and shrubs, dig a hole measuring roughly 60cm (2ft) square and refill it with a mixture of 50 per cent fresh loam and 50 per cent well-rotted organic matter. Apply this mixture every spring or autumn around the base of established plants.

Cover all the bare earth in a border to help retain moisture during dry periods.

SOIL

Soil is a mixture of mineral particles and organic matter. Air and water fill the spaces between, the water containing dissolved nutrients. In the soil live algae, bacteria and fungi, insects and worms. These feed on the organic matter and break it down, creating a rich, fertile soil in which seeds germinate and plants grow.

Soils are classified according to the varying amounts of sand, silt and clay they contain. Loam is an ideal blend of clay, silt and sand and is easily cultivated, retains moisture and suits most plants.

Clay consists of fine particles that cling together causing moisture retention – sticky when wet, shrinking and cracking in dry weather. Clay soils are not popular, being hard to work and slow to warm up

JANUARY ❧

in spring. However, they are rich and hold fertilizers well. They can be acid or alkaline − lime on acid clays can improve the texture, but is of no use on clays that are chalky or alkaline.

Sandy soils have large particles causing bigger air spaces so that water drains freely. Although sandy soils are easy to cultivate and warm up quickly in spring − making them good for early plants − they do dry out quickly and nutrients are washed out by rain or watering.

The explanation of pH

The formula pH is bandied about a lot although exactly what it means is not clearly understood by everyone; pH is a scale running from 0 to 14 used to measure the acid-alkaline balance of a soil. From 0 to 7 represent degrees of acidity (I would imagine hydrochloric acid would measure 0) and 7 to 14 represent degrees of alkalinity. When soils are described as being 'neutral', it is because they read 7 on the scale, neither acid nor alkaline. Most garden soils range between 6.5 and 7.5.

Soils are easily tested for pH with a simple kit bought at garden centres. It is not always necessary to buy one. If your neighbours' gardens are full of rhododendrons, azaleas, pieris and other acid-loving plants, then you can be pretty sure that your soil is on the acid side. If none of these plants appear in your area, your soil will be alkaline.

If you live in an alkaline area and you desperately want to grow acid-loving plants, you can do so in containers using ericaceous compost. Regular doses of products like Sequestrene or Miracid will boost a soil's acidity.

Organic matter

All three soil types benefit from attention: digging in well-rotted organic matter, or compost. In the case of heavy clay, grit and sharp

JANUARY

sand should also be added to help open it up further. Organic supplements should not be considered as a fertilizer as such, but rather something that improves soil structure, although they do give a degree of nourishment to plants, mainly in the form of nitrogen and useful bacteria. These are some of the best things to put on your soil:

❀ Farm-yard manure (FYM). Superb stuff that normally consists of horse droppings mixed with straw. It must be well-rotted. Always use FYM that is black and crumbly, from the bottom of the heap. It should not be used unless it is at least two years old.

❀ Spent mushroom compost. Should be composted for a year before use if it is to be dug into the soil. Being alkaline, it is not ideal for soils that are already alkaline, especially if it is applied regularly.

❀ Poultry manure. This contains a high percentage of nitrogen and should never be applied in concentrated form. It makes an excellent addition, in limited amounts, to the compost heap as a stimulator.

FASCINATING FACT

❀ Horses have one stomach, so grass seeds pass through and reappear still viable at the other end – in other words, fresh horse manure would spread grass and weeds all over your garden. However, composting generates sufficient heat to render the vast majority of grass seeds unviable (you may have seen steam rising from a dung heap on a cold day). Cattle have four stomachs, rendering grass seed unviable by the time it has passed through their systems. Dried cow pats therefore make excellent, nutritious additions to compost heaps.

HOME-MADE COMPOST

Recycling your own garden and kitchen waste makes sense, both from an environmental and a financial point of view.

What sort of bin?

You can buy compost bins from garden centres, or make your own. Organic matter decomposes all the quicker when the conditions are warm and damp, with only a certain amount of air allowed in. Bins should therefore be insulated on all sides as well as on top. There is no reason why a wire-mesh bin insulated with cardboard or newspaper on the inside should not work as efficiently as any other. They should not be larger than 1 x 1m (3 x 3ft) to allow a free passage of air throughout. Opinions vary as to the best materials for constructing a compost bin. I use wooden pallets, four at a time, tied together in a square with wire, with the close-slatted side on the inside.

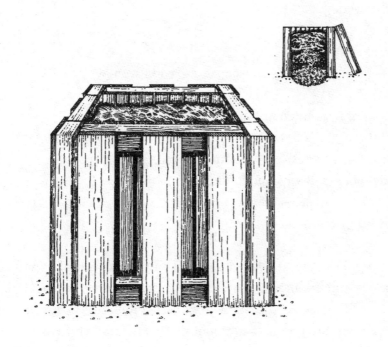

A compost bin made from wooden pallets.

Filling your compost bin

Ideally, you should fill a compost heap all in one go. Spray dry material with water from a watering can and cover the filled bin with an

JANUARY

old piece of carpet or something similar to keep the warmth in and the rain out. After about a week the compost should be turned with a garden fork, putting the material that was originally on the outside towards the centre. The compost should be ready after a further six months.

Put in your home-made compost:

grass clippings
vegetable kitchen waste
annual weeds
vegetable tops
dead flowers
tea bags
crushed egg shells
the occasional torn-up newspaper, mixed in well

Do not put in your compost:

meat, fat and bones, as they attract vermin
woody material (twigs and branches)
conifer and evergreen leaves
citrus fruit peelings

To help your compost decompose, you can add chemical stimulators. These are high in nitrogen to encourage the bacteria that break down the organic material. One of the very best stimulators is human urine, but you can buy products in liquid or pellet form, which is probably wiser in most circumstances. When you use any bought product in the garden, it is *vital* to adhere to the manufacturers' recommendations. Do not be tempted to overuse it in the belief that this will achieve a better result. By using a more concentrated dosage, you may be doing more harm than good. Add a stimulator near the bottom of your compost heap.

TIPS: MAKING COMPOST

❀ Never add too much of the same thing at once, as this tends to slow the rotting process down. Grass mowings are one of the worst offenders; if added in too thick a layer, they cut off the oxygen supply to the rest of the compost when they convert into a layer of gooey slime.

❀ Place your compost heap where it will receive some sunshine. This helps to warm it and accelerate the rotting process. Do not put it under an evergreen tree - for some reason they prove less efficient here.

❀ If you have the space, it is best to have three compost bins. One for filling, one for 'brewing' and one for use in the garden.

You can add fallen leaves in autumn to the compost heap. However, they can be successfully composted on their own in black refuse bags. Puncture the bags with a garden fork here and there to allow in some air and then stuff in as many leaves as you can, wetting them slightly if they are very dry before tying the top tightly. Beware: the fibrous leaves of the London Plane do not compost unless they are first shredded.

PLANTING IN WALLS

I am very lucky to have dry stone walls – they are the easiest in which to entertain certain plants. When I had mine rebuilt I asked the builder to leave the occasional gap close under the coping and to leave the middle (which would normally be filled with rubble) empty. I filled the space with a mixture of top soil and well-rotted organic matter, firming in as much as I could, before the next course of stone

❀ JANUARY

was laid. The result is a series of good, deep planting pockets with plenty of room for root expansion right into the middle of the wall. The organic matter will ensure that the soil remains damper in dry periods.

Brick walls do not lend themselves so readily to having plants growing in them, but if you are having a brick wall built, it is worth investigating the possibility of leaving some gaps in it, or leaving spaces between a double row of bricks to fill with soil and plants. Or, as I suggested in the section on raised beds (see page 71) you could set small terracotta, up-turned pots in gaps in brick walls for small plants.

Plants for growing in walls

Some plants are better adapted to growing in walls than others. Surprisingly, common buddleia will seed itself almost anywhere and can grow enormous in an old brick wall, despite the fact that there appears to be precious little room for its roots. It was a common sight growing in the walls of bombed buildings in the years following the war and can still be seen on derelict buildings today. Most wall plants are, of course, much smaller.

Plants for sunny walls are:

Aubretia. Flowers in blue, purple or red in spring. Grows into large cascading cushions if planted in a border at the top of a supporting wall, but can also oblige in the meanest crack.

Alyssum montanum. Masses of yellow, scented flowers in summer.

Cerastium tomentosum (Snow in summer). Silver foliage and white flowers in summer.

Erodium chrysanthum. Silvery stems and fern-like leaves and sprays of creamy-yellow flowers in late spring and summer.

Lewisia, Cotyledon hybrids. Evergreen rosettes of toothed leaves and clusters of beautiful flowers of many different colours in early summer. Perfectly happy on its side when grown in a wall.

JANUARY ❧

Plants for shaded walls are:

Arabis caucasica. Fragrant white or pink flowers in late spring and
   summer.
Corydalis lutea. An evergreen with slender yellow flowers that will
   grow practically anywhere.
Cymbalaria muralis (Ivy-leaved toadflax). Small, ivy-shaped, pale
   green leaves and masses of tiny, tubular, white flowers in summer.
Phyllitis scolopendrium (also called *Asplenium scolopendrium*).
   An evergreen fern that grows very happily on a shaded wall
   especially if it is damp.
Polystichum setiferum (Soft shield fern). A most obliging evergreen
   or semi-evergreen fern.
Saxifraga hirsuta (Saxifrage). Panacles of tiny, star-shaped white
   flowers in late spring and early summer.

Cuttings of most alpines will take root if pushed into crevices of dry
stone walls, with a little soil added first, in spring or autumn.

FENCING

The sort of fence you choose depends on personal taste and its sur-
roundings. In my country garden, I chose wattle fencing panels, for
instance, but they might look too rough and rustic in town gardens.
Some of the kinds of fencing you can get are:

❀ rustic fencing
❀ willow wattle panels
❀ hazel wattle panels; these are easily wired onto round stakes.
❀ reed panels (made with reeds cut from the Norfolk Broads and the
Suffolk coast). These are edged with wooden strips around all four
sides and cost about the same as wattle panels. They are either
screwed or nailed onto square posts. Both hazel wattle and reed panels
last for about twenty-five years and will filter strong winds.

JANUARY

❀ Ordinary fencing includes larch lap panels, which are cheaper than the rustic kinds but do not last as long, and closeboard fencing. These are best screwed onto square posts.

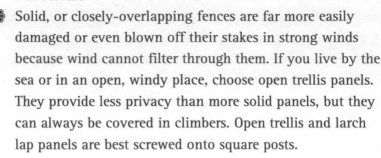

> TIP: FENCES
>
> ❀ Solid, or closely-overlapping fences are far more easily damaged or even blown off their stakes in strong winds because wind cannot filter through them. If you live by the sea or in an open, windy place, choose open trellis panels. They provide less privacy than more solid panels, but they can always be covered in climbers. Open trellis and larch lap panels are best screwed onto square posts.

Putting up a fence

Putting up fences is quite an art and you may prefer to get someone to do it for you. If you want to try doing it yourself, here are the basic principles.

You will need one post more than the number of panels. Allow for stakes or posts to go 60cm (2ft) into the ground. For example, if the fence is to be 2m (6ft) high, you will need 2.5m (8ft) stakes or posts. If, for aesthetic reasons, you are not treating the whole fence with wood preservative, at least treat the section of the post that will go underground.

> WARNING
>
> ❀ If you want to erect a fence higher than 2m (6ft), you may need to get planning permission first from your local council.

Measure out and dig holes 60cm (2ft) deep at the correct spacing. Put a post in each hole. Drop a few stones down the hole to stabilize it, then fill in with soil and tamp down with your heel very firmly. (Depending on the type of fencing you are erecting, you may wish to use metal stakes to fit your poles into, or to fill the holes with concrete for extra stability.) Fasten the fencing panels to the posts with the appropriate fixings for your type of fence. Finish off the posts with finials – these make all the difference.

TOOLS

January is a good month to clean and oil tools before they are put away in a dry place for the rest of the winter. Without tools a gardener is sunk and so it is far better to make sure they're all in good condition now, rather than finding you cannot use them when you really need them. There is no reason why tools that are well cared for should not last a lifetime. This is also a good time to paint the handles of tools you are always losing, like trowels, with a bright colour.

Tools should be cleaned after use as a matter of course; there's nothing worse than picking up a spade caked in mud. Before they are put away for the winter, many metal tools can be given a clean by being moved up and down in a mixture of old car oil and sharp sand in a bucket – an old, tried and tested method. Wooden handles should be treated with linseed oil. Excessive rust can be cleaned off using a proprietory product and other dirty tools can be cleaned with oven cleaner using a toothbrush.

Tools are just like shoes: the more you pay for them and the better you look after them, the longer they will last. More expensive tools, especially in the case of spades and forks, are made so that their weak point, where the handle meets the blade, has extra reinforcement.

Before you buy heavier tools like spades and forks, make sure they feel comfortable to handle and that they are not too heavy.

SPADE

This is needed for digging deep holes for planting and moving trees

JANUARY

and shrubs, or for improving soil structure when organic matter is added to the soil at a depth of two spits. If you garden in rubber boots it is best to choose a spade with flattened treads.

FORK

This is required for lifting root crops, manually aerating lawns, moving compost and breaking up surface clods of earth.

RAKE

There are basically two sorts of rake. The garden rake with short metal teeth for preparing seed beds and soil levelling and the 'springbok' type, with longer, springier teeth for raking lawns and clearing up debris.

HOE

Hoes come in different shapes and sizes. The Dutch hoe, with a head shaped like a horseshoe and a flat band of metal along the open end, is effective and easy to use especially if the blade is sharp.

TROWEL

It is worth your while investing in a good trowel, with a stainless steel blade for moving small plants around the garden and weeding in awkward places. Cheap trowels soon bend and break.

SECATEURS

There is a bewildering range of secateurs, none of which should never be used for cutting living wood thicker than a finger. (Thicker stems should be cut with loppers or a small saw that folds back into its handle.) Secateurs are all too easily strained when used on dead wood after which they will never be the same again. There are basically two different types of secateur: the 'parrot beak' with a scissor action and the 'anvil'. Both will last a lifetime if treated with respect, never allowed to cut anything too large and kept sharpened and oiled. Buy secateurs with coloured handles to prevent you from losing them.

JANUARY ❁

KNIFE

I never go out into the garden without a knife and green string in my pocket. There is always something that needs tying or cutting. These two and a great many other useful little things like a hammer, packets of seeds, nails and wire, can all be carried in a tool belt around the waist.

Sharp knives with blades of empered steel that fold back into wooden handles, sold as budding or grafting knives, are invaluable for dozens of jobs including taking cuttings and cutting string. Always keep a whetstone in the potting shed to keep your knife as sharp as a razor.

SHEARS

These are indispensable for giving haircuts to plants like lavender, heather and aubretia once their flowers have faded. Clean the blades with emery paper after use and keep them well oiled.

DIBBER

This is invaluable for planting out seedlings. It can be made from the broken wooden handle of an old fork or spade.

PICK-AXE AND SLEDGEHAMMER

A pick-axe comes in very useful for the removal of roots of dead trees and shrubs, as does a sledgehammer for the removal of old stumps.

WHEELBARROW

This is indispensable – try to find a make without an inflatable tyre on the wheel as these are always going flat!

The tools in the potting shed – your pride and joy

The best way of storing tools is to arrange them on a smooth dark-coloured wall on nails. Once you are satisfied with their arrangement,

JANUARY

draw around them with a pencil and paint in their shapes using white paint. This is the best way of knowing when a tool is missing – when all there is to see is the white shape of the tool.

CLOTHES

As I continue to hack my way through the remaining impenetrable jungle of the rest of the garden, that will one day be tamed, I bless my industrial overalls. I seldom, if ever, get scratched by brambles, or stung by nettles and I feel safe – as if I am going into battle protected by armour. Similarly, I wear tough gardening gloves for practically every job except mowing. I wear sturdy leather-soled boots whenever I have a lot of digging to do and my spade does not have a flattened top to the spit which can dig into rubber soles.

TIPS: SAFETY

❀ Always wear goggles when strimming and using electric hedge trimmers.

❀ All electrically driven garden machinery should be plugged into a circuit breaker.

❀ Young children can drown in very shallow water. See page 135 for an idea for a child-safe pond.

JANUARY TASKS

❀ Keep a rake handy by the garden door to use for knocking snow off plants like bamboos and evergreen conifers whose limbs can be damaged by the weight of snow.

❀ Float a rubber ball or a few logs in ornamental, concrete-lined ponds to prevent expanding ice from cracking the superstructure.

❀ Sprinkle wood ash onto slippery paths to avoid nasty accidents. Tack chicken wire onto wooden surfaces for the same reason.

JANUARY

❀ Cut away the plumes of Pampas grass at the base as they are beginning to look tatty. Wear gloves and protective clothing against the abrasive leaves.

❀ Start planning the position of crops in the vegetable garden. The same crop should never be grown in the same place two years running in order to reduce the likelihood of disease.

❀ Remove faded flowers on indoor flowering cyclamen by giving them a good tug.

❀ Put indoor flowering Indian azaleas in a cool conservatory or greenhouse to prolong flowering.

❀ Support the flowers on floppy hyacinths grown indoors on taut green string tied to small canes arranged around the pot.

❀ Make sure the birds have something to eat and drink. They will pay you back in the summer months by eating unwanted pests like caterpillars.

❀ Take 15cm (6 inch) cuttings of ivy in any average soil.

❀ JANUARY

Dark days before spring

I AM SOMETIMES REFERRED TO AS AN EXPERT, which means that I must know absolutely *everything* about horticulture and its associated subjects. Well, I do not. I do not even pretend to, nor can anyone in my profession. After all, there are thousands of named roses and apples, of which I recognize some but by no means all and I do not know everything about pests and diseases, my Achilles heel. Further, it is impossible for one person to know the botanic names of every living plant. If there is such a person, let him or her stand and be tested!

Horticulture, like medicine, is a multifaceted subject. There's design, commercial (the production of food and nursery stock), amenity (the management of public and private gardens), pathology (the study of plant diseases), arboriculture (the study of trees and tree surgery), botany, organic gardening, even garden history, to mention but a few and if you specialize in one it is useful to have some knowledge of the others. Unlike medicine, however, few can afford to specialize in plant pathology only, for example. In an ideal world I would like the time to improve my tree knowledge as there are still so many I do not know, mainly because I have never grown them. Later perhaps I could specialize in one genus like *Quercus* (oak).

A LOAD OF OLD MANURE

Everyone, including me, talks about the importance of well-rotted farm-yard manure as an essential addition to the soil (see page 84). Of course we are all absolutely right, but I have to admit, ruefully, that it is not quite so straightforward when you actually go out and search for it – even in a rural area like my own, it is not that easy to find. Here I am, perched on the edge of the Cotswolds with open country on all sides, the fields groaning with horses and cattle, yet the well-rotted stuff is proving elusive.

Several telephone calls to local farmers produced negative responses as it is their way to spread muck on their fields before it has properly rotted down. The best bet, I have since discovered, is to ask people who have stables, who *sometimes* have some if it has not already been promised to someone else. There's a new fashion to bed down horses with recycled newspaper, expensive at over £3 a bag, but it has the advantage of rotting down faster than straw-based bedding. I have managed to acquire a bag or two of this, but I need very much more. I prefer cow-based muck as it contains little viable grass seed.

When I was a boy we had a gardener called Mr Williams who used to make liquid plant food in the old-fashioned way. He used to seep a hessian sack full of sheep droppings in a tank of water for a few months. The resulting brown liquid, when applied to vegetables, produced wonders. I must try it this summer. By the way, did you know that about the only seed to pass through the human system unscathed is that of the tomato? Now there's something you can bring up at a dinner party when conversation becomes sticky.

THE DOVECOTE

At the gable end of the house, facing the loose boxes which I have converted into my office, there sit three old rusty oil tanks. Oil I have to have in order to feed the throbbing heart of the house, the Aga, and so I have replaced the tanks with a new state-of-the-art plastic one. It is positioned in the centre of the wall and will later be camouflaged somehow. Directly above it a wooden, white-painted, wall-mounted dovecote now takes pride of place.

The basics of 'homing' a pair of doves are as follows: first of all you have to find a compatible pair, who prove, dare I say, lovey-dovey. They are difficult to sex and therefore they must be bought from a specialist supplier. They will give you a pair that have already shown interest in each other but even this is not foolproof, as doves of the same sex are almost as prone to do this as a pair of opposites. You will know if you have a true pair, as they soon start to breed and produce a new lot of chicks, normally two at a time, every eight weeks thereafter.

They need to be confined to the dovecote initially for about one month with the help of a small cage annexe and need to be fed every day thereafter. It also helps to supply water and their boxes need cleaning out twice yearly. They should not be netted in during the initial period as netting can stress and snare them. You start with one pair whose offspring, you hope, will return 'home' to nest in one of the other cotes (I have three).

When we moved to the house there were several specimens of *Cotoneaster horizontalis*, a plant I have always found gloomy in the extreme, so I took great delight in digging them up. I have also inherited some tree-like cotoneasters (*C. frigidus* 'Cornubia') which have so much more oomph and character than their miserable sprawling cousin. I have thinned the tall-growing ones to upward-growing shoots and they look very fine. Bees love all cotoneasters.

The lesson of the Bishop of Llandaff

The more you garden, the more fascinating it all becomes. As your plant knowledge improves you can start to pick and choose species and cultivars from every genus, the dahlia 'The Bishop of Llandaff' being an excellent case in point. My uncle had a splendid old butler

FEBRUARY

called Adams who thought it vulgar to provide ice for drinks in the drawing room because he considered it a vulgar American habit. Adams used to win first prize every year at the Great Somerford Show for his dahlias, his pride and joy. These were huge mophead affairs in bronze, muddy pink and dirty yellow and fond as I was of their grower, they always made me wince, even at the tender age of ten or thereabouts. They left such a strong feeling of revulsion that I dismissed them as too nasty to contemplate ever again, but then the good bishop came into my life. His gorgeous, dark red, single flowers and bronze foliage combine to make a striking combination that no mixed border should be without.

TIME TO BROWSE

As I write, ten days into February, the ground is still frozen solid and has been so with very few days' grace since New Year's Day. It is very frustrating as I cannot finish the levelling and start on the trenching. When I rang up to cancel my JCB the contractor confirmed it would have been a waste of time. 'My machines are picking up wheelbarrow-size chunks of frozen ground.'

It is during periods like this that time can be spent usefully thumbing through seed catalogues. To cheer yourself up, branches of forsythia and flowering currant can be cut and put into a bucket of water for early forcing in the house.

BIRDS IN THE GARDEN

I feel that my doves are a soothing and attractive addition to a garden but birdsong and the flash of bright feathers are a welcome addition anywhere. If a dovecote is beyond your reach, you can still do a lot to make your garden attractive to birds and so enjoy their company. In the stark winter months, it is a joy, too, to feed our native friends who may be finding life hard and food scarce. They can cheer you up

FEBRUARY ❦

with their sprightly activity in the dead winter garden. Some resident birds, such as insectivorous blue tits and great tits, will also help to keep black fly and other pest populations down. Some ways to attract birds into your garden are to install a bird table, put up nesting boxes and grow plants that birds can feed from.

Bird tables

These can be built quite easily by the amateur carpenter by making a roofed platform sitting on the top of a pole at least 2m (6ft) high. The pole can be sheathed with PVC piping to prevent domestic cats, garden birds' worst enemy, from climbing up it. Because birds like space between each other when feeding, the platform should be no smaller than 40cm (15in) square. You can buy bird tables at no great cost, too. It is a lovely present to buy or make for someone, particularly someone fairly immobile who can enjoy all the visitors from a convenient window. It is best to have it built by late summer to give your garden birds enough time to get used to it before winter sets in.

A well-stocked bird table will attract welcome visitors to your garden.

❦ FEBRUARY

Put cheese, bacon rind, bread and chopped apple on your bird table. Attach a hanging feeder to the edge. Fill it with black sunflower seed or top-grade peanuts for the tits and finches. Peanuts should be top-grade for feeding birds, otherwise they can prove toxic. Always buy them from a reputable pet shop.

It is best to phase out feeding the birds as spring arrives, so that they eat more of the natural foods which give them the nourishment they require. This will also encourage the young birds to learn to fend for themselves.

WARNING BELLS

Domestic cats are responsible for the death of millions of birds a year. If you are a lover of both cats and birds, attach a small bell on your cat's collar to give birds some warning of approaching danger.

Birds also need water, not only to drink, but also for bathing, in order to keep their feathers clean. Dirty feathers do not ensure efficient insulation on cold winter nights. A pond with a gently sloping bank (see wildlife ponds, page 140) is ideal, otherwise a bird bath is an excellent alternative. Although the water needs to be changed regularly, as clean water is essential to a bathing bird's happiness, a bird bath within comfortable view of a window gives you a far better view of the birds themselves. Watching a bird bathe is so much more entertaining than any television programme I have ever watched. The biggest problem with bird baths is that they freeze solid in winter, sometimes for weeks. If you want to provide birds with 5-star accommodation, you could submerge an electric pond heater in the water.

Plants for birds

There is a wide range of plants, from trees to annual flowers, that provide a natural food source for birds, either in the form of fruits

(berries) or seed heads. As a general rule, birds prefer plants that produce red berries as opposed to yellow or orange.

Here's a selection of plants and trees that will keep the birds
happy in your garden.

TREES

Alnus glutinosa 'Aurea' (Golden alder). More decorative than the
common alder, this is a conical tree with bright yellow leaves
turning pale green in summer. A useful tree for a boggy soil, it
supplies an abundant crop of seeds in autumn much favoured by
redpolls and siskins, as well as blue tits, marsh tits, coal tits and
great tits.

Crataegus monogyna (Common hawthorn). A familiar hedgerow plant
with glorious display of white blossom in May followed by red
haws (berries) loved by blackbirds, thrushes and finches as well as
the winter-visiting redwings and fieldfares.

Malus tschonoskii (Crab apple). Most birds love the fruit of all the
crab apples but this is a more ornamental species better suited to a
domestic garden. Red-flushed, yellowish-green fruits are followed
by rich autumn tints of orange, red and purple.

Prunus avium (Wild cherry). Not suitable for small gardens as it
grows too large. The white blossoms in spring attract insects which
in turn attract birds like warblers. This is a favourite of bullfinches
who love the juicy fruits in late summer.

Prunus padus (Bird cherry). A smaller tree than the Wild cherry,
whose fruits attract many different birds.

Sorbus aucuparia (Rowan, Mountain ash). White flowers in spring
are followed by clusters of red berries in autumn.

SHRUBS

Cotoneaster horizontalis. A low, spreading bush with small red berries
in autumn.

Cotoneaster x watereri. An evergreen or semi-evergreen large shrub
or small tree with arching branches bearing white flowers in early

FEBRUARY

summer followed in autumn by prolific, large clusters of red berries.

Euonymus europaeus 'Red Cascade' (Spindle tree). Prolific red berries in autumn joined by red foliage.

Mahonia aquifolium (Oregon Grape). Evergreen shrub with small scented yellow flowers in spring followed by blue-black berries in autumn. Able to thrive in drought conditions and prefers a slightly acid soil.

Pyracantha atalantoides (Firethorn). A very useful shrub where space is limited as it can be trained tight up a wall or fence. A favourite with redwings for its red berries in autumn. Also *P. coccinea* whose red berries can persist as late as February.

Viburnum opulus (Guelder rose). Produces prolific red fruits in autumn. Its beautiful variety *V. o. sterile*, the Snowball Bush, does not produce berries for birds as its name suggests. Best in limey soils.

FLOWERS FOR SEED

There are a number of perennials, biennials and annuals that supply food for birds with their seed heads. These include candytuft for greenfinches; cornflowers, corn marigolds and forget-me-nots for finches; honesty and cranesbill for bullfinches; Scotch thistle (*Onopordum acanthium*), teasel and Michaelmas daisies for goldfinches. Also cardoon (*Cynara cardunculus*) and globe artichoke (*C. scolymus*).

NESTING BOXES

Birds like to build their nests in thick, evergreen plants like ivy and conifers that give them cover, but they will also take readily to man-made nesting boxes. They come in different shapes and sizes, designed to attract a particular species while preventing others from using the same box. It is best to install nesting boxes during the winter to give birds enough time to get used to them before the breeding season begins.

FEBRUARY ❁

Nesting boxes can be attached to trees, walls or fences, from 2-5m (6-16 feet) above the ground, preferably facing between northeast and southeast to avoid the midday sun and the wettest winds.

PEST CONTROL

Every gardener wages an ongoing battle against enemies who are often invisible, yet are highly efficient in distorting leaves and shoots, spoiling flowers and fruit and causing the death of many plants. Healthy, strong plants are better armed to withstand the attacks of pests and diseases and some insects and birds should be encouraged to join your side in the battle.

Although, in the case of plant diseases, prevention is better than cure, blanket spraying with chemicals is not desirable from an environmental point of view. Try to use chemicals only when absolutely necessary and then sparingly. If you use a chemical treatment that might also be harmful to beneficial insects like bees, spray very early in the morning, or very late in the evening when the insects are not active. Choose a time when the foliage is dry and the air still. Many systemic insecticides are derived from plants and are applied to foliage to become absorbed into the plant's system. Such sprays are fatal only to those insects that feed on the plant's leaves, stems or sap and does not affect pollinating insects except at the time of application, thus they are less damaging to the environment as a whole. Contact sprays however, are non-selective and kill both pests and beneficial insects. Both contact sprays and non-systemic fungicides are short-lived. Many of these are derived from plants and have a less damaging effect on the environment as a whole than all-embracing chemical pesticides and fungicides.

Environmental friends

A healthy garden with a wide range of plants will attract many forms of wildlife including natural predators such as birds, ladybirds,

FEBRUARY

hedgehogs, frogs and toads. Their presence will help to maintain a naturally balanced environment and the need for artificial pest control will be kept to a minimum. Regular hoeing between plants will not only control weeds but bring many pests to the surface where birds can deal with them. The following are some of a gardener's friends:

❀ Anthocoris bugs. These are 2mm ($1/6$in) long and black-brown. They often gather on willow catkins and eat insects, capsid bugs, caterpillars and midges.

❀ Birds. Help to control grubs, snails, slugs, caterpillars and aphids.

❀ Centipedes. Shelter below ground cover during the day and at night prey on many small insects and slugs.

❀ Frogs and toads. Will keep the slug population down and also eat woodlice – a good reason for considering a water feature, where they can breed, in your garden.

❀ Ground beetles. Like damp, shaded places by day, but at night hunt for eelworms, leatherjackets, larvae and insect eggs.

❀ Hedgehogs. Will forage for slugs, cutworms, wireworms, woodlice and millipedes at night.

❀ Hover flies. These thin, wasp-like insects lay their eggs on aphid colonies. The larvae have voracious appetites and are very effective in keeping aphid populations down. French marigolds and poached-egg plants attract hover flies.

❀ Lacewings. Produce larvae that suck body fluids from aphids. In theory, the larvae from just one female could consume 20 million aphids in one season, although of course they are themselves the prey of some of the above.

❀ Ladybirds. Feed on aphids when they are at both larvae and adult stages. They also consume scale insects, mealy bugs, thrips and mites.

The following are safe to spray:

❀ Copper fungicides. Such as Bordeaux and Burgundy mixtures, remain effective for several weeks as a control against mildew and blight, although they are harmless to most insects.

❀ Derris. Is a plant extract for killing caterpillars and aphids. It is toxic to the eggs of ladybirds and to adult lacewings and so should be used carefully.

❀ Insecticidal soap. This has a potassium base and is effective only for a day at a time. However, a direct hit kills aphids, red spider mites, whiteflies, scale insects and mealy bugs.

❀ Pyrethrum and Rotenone. Extracted from the flowers of certain chrysanthemums, these are harmful to some beneficial insects, but they are short-lived. They should be carefully directed at pests such as aphids.

❀ Quassia. Is sold in chip form, simmered in water and strained before use. It controls small caterpillars and aphids without harming bees, ladybirds or anthocoris bugs.

FEBRUARY TASKS

❀ Clean out the cold frame and sow early lettuce and beetroot.

❀ Continue to plant trees and shrubs in mild spells, but mulch around their base to protect their shallow root systems from penetrating frosts.

❀ Clean out the potting shed and arrange garden tools. Potting sheds should be tidy and welcoming places. Sharpen knives and other cutting tools including spades. Oil all metal blades and moving parts to prevent them from rusting.

❀ Get the lawn mower serviced in plenty of time before the spring. If you book your mower in now you are less likely to have to wait in the queue with everyone else who thinks about getting the mower serviced in the spring.

❀ Protect plants from hungry mice in cold frames. If you do not like the idea of killing mice, there do exist 'humanitarian' traps.

❀ Order flower seed, lily bulbs and plug plants from catalogues. Remember to keep a photocopy of your order form just in case they never materialize.

❀ FEBRUARY

❀ Mulch around the base of young ornamental and fruit trees with well-rotted organic matter to aid moisture retention in the soil during dry spells in summer.

❀ At the end of the month, cut back overgrown hedges in order to reshape them.

❀ Sweep worm casts off the lawn with a besom. If they are trodden on they can clog and damage turf.

❀ Be careful not to stand on emerging spring bulbs, especially where they are planted in turf.

❀ Trim the faded flowers of winter-flowering heathers with shears to tidy them up.

FEBRUARY ❀

Humour in the garden

MARCH

ROSIE, MY YOUNGEST, eight-year-old daughter with flaming red hair and temper to match, has been busy planting seeds, which I have put on a window sill in the kitchen. She has planted asters, schizanthus and eschscholzias and four tomatoes. It is a pleasure watching her taking such an interest in gardening. I'll choose a sunny spot where the soil is good for these plants, to make sure they thrive. She may, if her confidence is sufficiently boosted this time, try again next year. I like to think it is in her blood.

It seems to freeze all the time. The ground is like concrete, meaning that gardening has come to a standstill. The spring bulbs are hardly showing.

THE TOPIARY FARMYARD

Gardens should contain at least one amusing feature. So much thought goes into colour harmony in the herbaceous border, the perfect juxtapositioning of plants, the right scale for the pond and pergola and so on, that often humour is forgotten. I want people to smile with me in my garden and so I am planning a topiary farm-yard scene in the front of the house. The area by the front door is difficult to design as it sits close-in underneath the north side of the house where the walls are high and therefore the shade intense except in mid-summer. There is an open drain running round the outside of the house which is going to present problems when it comes to planting climbers. Yes, of course there are several shade-tolerant shrubs and climbers but practically all of them do so much better given more light. I didn't want to collect and feature shade-tolerant plants as such, so another solution had to be found.

My eyes were first opened to the idea of topiary figures back in 1980 when I saw some wonderful examples in Hollywood, California. A garden designer there was planning to plant a garden in a woodland setting with all the characters from *A Midsummer Night's Dream*. The frames for the topiary animals can be bought, from small piglets to life-size horses, which are made in galvanized steel rods and wire, perfect for common box and yew. I also want to include some ivy sculptures and these are best trained over chicken-wire frames which I shall attempt to make myself. I know for certain I want a pig and some chickens and a nest in ivy complete with some china eggs.

When we got here this small garden consisted of neglected gravelly ground, with great swathes of Snow in summer (*Cerastium*) and self-sown primroses in amongst the weeds. One of the first things I did when I got here was to realign the wall which used to guide clients to the front door (when the house was a pub, I hasten to add). The wall now runs parallel to the house, at a respectful distance. I was determined right from the word go to have my hollyhock hedge close to the wall, but it was difficult to decide how to fill the space between it and the house.

The solution then came to me. Writing a national newspaper gardening column every Sunday, I get to meet a great many interesting people. They nourish my mind and broaden my horizons. One of them, Elizabeth Baimbridge, has an interesting story to tell. She wanted to buy some dwarf box plants back in 1980 and had great difficulty in sourcing them, so she decided to grow some herself. Now

MARCH ✿

known as 'Madame Buxus' in France, 'The Boxwood Lady' in England and 'La Madrina de Buxus' in Cuba (surprisingly, 24 species of box are native to Cuba), she has built up the largest box nursery in Europe in a mere decade or so. Inspired by Elizabeth Baimbridge, I now plan to surround my topiary animals within formal dwarf box hedging and I may resort to *Cerastium* as an in-fill, or gravel perhaps. The ground slopes slightly in this area so I am using scaffolding planks secured with pegs to get the levels right.

TRULY HARDY SHRUBS

My first winter in my new village has been a tough one and it has made me aware of the importance of choosing hardy trees and shrubs. We are certainly very exposed up here. A local told me the other day that there was nothing between us and the Urals and soon afterwards I heard Natasha, my second daughter (now 11), telling someone that there was nothing between us and the 'urinals'.

After a lot of research wading through books to find hardy trees and shrubs that I like, I happened to stumble across one of the most unprepossessing-looking little books in my library called *Award of Garden Merit Plants*, published by the RHS. It turned out to be a mine of information. Consisting of botanic plants lists in alphabetical order, this booklet succeeded in completing my research in no time. All plants that appear in the booklet, and there are thousands of them in several categories, including hardy herbaceous plants, fruit and vegetables, alpines and conservatory plants, have been vetted by the RHS. In their own words '[This booklet] recognizes plants of outstanding excellence for garden decoration or use.'

From this booklet I have chosen shrubs like *Cotinus* 'Grace' and *Parrotia persica* for their autumn tints and *Mahonia* x *media* 'Charity' and *Garrya elliptica* 'James Roof' for their contribution in winter. Trees include *Syringa vulgaris* 'Madame Lemoine' – surely the best of the white-flowering lilacs – *Robinia* x *fraseri* 'Red Robin' for its red leaves in spring and *Liquidamber styraciflua* 'Worplesdon' for its

❧ MARCH

autumn tints.

This no-nonsense booklet is now sitting on a shelf reserved for books I find I use most, like *The Plant Finder, The Hillier Manual of Trees and Shrubs, Roget's Thesaurus, Chambers Twentieth Century Dictionary* and Graham Stuart Thomas's *Ornamental Shrubs, Climbers and Bamboos* and *Perennial Garden Plants*.

The bitterly cold easterly winds have returned bringing snow with them. Last night the wind blew snow right into the barn, covering my logs and spare carpets. It is enough to make a chap spit with rage.

TOPIARY

'Topiary' is the word used to describe a plant clipped to a particular shape, an art form known to have been used in Ancient Rome. There are many plants that can be clipped into a large variety of different shapes to form bold features and there's nearly always a place for at least one in every garden. A clipped evergreen shape becomes a living statue that maintains interest even during winter. Topiary is not a difficult art to master so long as you can exercise patience initially and are prepared to keep them in shape once they're established. The end result is always worth the wait.

A touch of humour

Topiary shapes can be simple or ornate according to your whim. I chose farm-yard animals close to the front door of my house to add a touch of humour as you arrive. I have seen different humorous ideas, mostly outside village cottages, also sitting in full view in front of the house. Peacocks, cake-stands and teddy-bears are a popular choice although I have also seen giant snails, even a battleship. I have also seen a hunting scene of two mounted horses at full gallop preceded by a few hounds and a fox, a scaled down Eiffel Tower and an oversized elephant forming a walk-through arch under its tummy!

Formal shapes

Formal settings often demand formal topiary using more simple geometric shapes, such as obelisks, pyramids, cones, balls, squares, spirals, mushrooms and lollipops.

Use formal or geometric shapes for formal parterres (see page 22), in amongst patterned borders edged in dwarf box (*Buxus semper-virens* 'Suffruticosa') and in containers on either side of a doorway or gate.

Plants to use for topiary

All plants that can be shaped for topiary are those also used for ornamental hedging. Common yew (*Taxus baccata*) is normally used for large topiary specimens because of the strength of its wood. Common box (*Buxus sempervirens*) is ideally used for smaller geometric shapes for the same reason and both need only be clipped once a year in August. All the following plants are hardy:

E = Evergreen S/E = Semi-Evergreen AGR = Approximate Growth Rate per annum TT = Time to Trim ST = Shade Tolerant SEC = best clipped using secateurs as opposed to shears (referring to plants with larger leaves).

Buxus sempervirens 'Handsworthensis' (variety of Common box)
E AGR30cm (1ft) TT early summer, ST. Vigorous, with dark green leaves. There are also many other different forms of box of different shades of green as well as glaucous blue and variegated foliage.

x *Cupressocyparis leylandii* (Leyland cypress) E AGR60cm (2ft)
TT May, late June and late August. I am hesitant to suggest this plant as it is often allowed to grow unchecked, resulting in neighbourly feuds. Increasingly popular because it is the fastest-growing evergreen, it *must* be kept regularly clipped during the summer. Useful for framing windows and doors.

❈ MARCH

Hedera (Ivy) E AGR slow to begin with then 30cm (1ft) TT whenever necessary, ST SEC. The smaller-leaved ivies are used to clothe preformed wire shapes, e.g., chickens or dogs that are first stuffed with moss.

Ilex aquifolium (Common English holly) E AGR30cm (1ft) TT spring or August, ST SEC. Best used for large geometric shapes. Many useful variegated cultivars for bold splashes of shades of yellow and silver. Prickly.

Ligustrum ovalifolium (privet) S/E AGR30cm (1ft) TT spring, mid and late summer. Best suited to being cut into large spheres. *L. o* 'Aurea' is the golden form.

Prunus lusitanica (Portugal laurel) E AGR30cm (1ft) TT spring and summer, SEC. Perfect for clipping into umbrellas and mopheads on tall bare trunks.

Pyracantha (Firethorn) S/E AGR30cm (1ft) TT any time from spring to autumn. Very useful plant for training up walls, to frame windows and doors.

Taxus baccata (Common or English yew) E AGR30cm (1ft) TT August, ST. This is the most popularly used evergreen for both topiary and hedges. Yew's reputation for being slow-growing is not the case if it is kept well watered and fed, especially during its first couple of seasons. Also golden and variegated forms.

Taxus baccata 'Fastigiata' (Irish yew) E. AGR30cm (1ft) TT August, ST. Vertically growing shoots resulting in a naturally columnar shape. Also a golden sun-loving form. Used very effectively planted either side of a gateway, or in two straight lines some distance from each other as a small avenue.

Training plants onto a frame

You can either make the frames yourself or buy them ready-made in a variety of shapes. When it comes to larger animals such as my pig, common box (*Buxus sempervirens*) is a perfect plant to use, with one plant positioned at the base of each leg, planted in the ground.

MARCH

STARTING A TOPIARY SHAPE

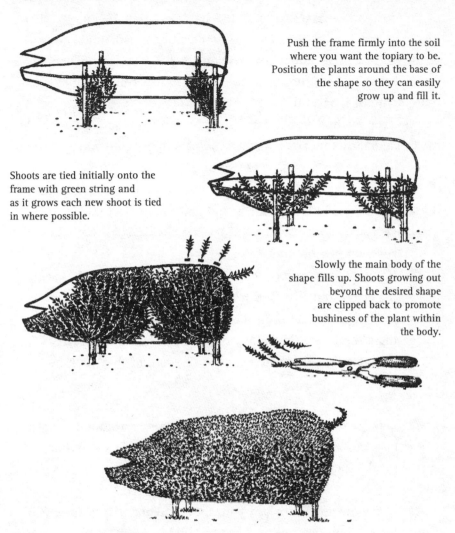

Push the frame firmly into the soil where you want the topiary to be. Position the plants around the base of the shape so they can easily grow up and fill it.

Shoots are tied initially onto the frame with green string and as it grows each new shoot is tied in where possible.

Slowly the main body of the shape fills up. Shoots growing out beyond the desired shape are clipped back to promote bushiness of the plant within the body.

MARCH

This process continues until the desired shape is achieved by clipping to the contours of the frame. This will take about four years.

With smaller shapes, like my chickens, use sphagnum moss, a little potting compost and small-leaved ivies (*Hedera helix* species) for outside use and creeping fig (*Ficus pumila*) for indoors. Stuff the body tightly with dampened sphagnum moss starting with the extremities, wrapping each tightly with clear fishing line as you go. Clip the moss smooth with scissors. Place the whole into a pot or the ground and plant four or five ivies around the base, pinning down the shoots onto the shape with florist's pins. Inevitably it will look patchy to begin with. It takes about one season for the ivies to cover a small frame depending on the size of the plants used. Trim and pin regularly to maintain shape.

Another method is to plant the ivies into the sphagnum within the frame but this means that the moss has to be sprayed regularly to keep it damp and is therefore not so practical.

You could plant a small topiary shape in a pot, using creeping fig (*Ficus pumila*) for indoors. This would make a lovely present.

TOPIARY DESIGN TIPS

❁ If you have a topiary shape in a pot and you want to keep the effect, but it suffers from dryness, remove the base of the pot and stand it on the garden soil. It sends roots into the ground and the plant can get all the moisture it needs. Keep plants clipped to a certain size so that they look in scale with their pot.

❁ Four plants of common box can be planted around the base of a tree and later clipped to make it look like a container for the tree.

❁ Mix variegated forms of your topiary plant with plain green forms, to enrich your palette and add interest.

HEDGES

Any of the above topiary plants make excellent hedges. There are further hedging plants, not as well suited to being clipped into fancy shapes, that need to be mentioned. These are planted about 45cm

(18in) apart in either single or, if a thicker hedge is wanted, double or staggered rows.

Carpinus betulus (Hornbeam) AGR30cm (1ft) TT August. Very similar
    in appearance to common beech (see below). Unlike beech it grows
    in heavy clay and retains its dead leaves in winter.
Crataegus monogyna (Common hawthorn) AGR30cm (1ft) TT when
    necessary between early summer and autumn. Eventually makes
    an impenetrable, thorny hedge.
Fagus sylvatica (Common beech) AGR30cm (1ft) TT August. Retains
    its dead leaves in winter and sheds them in spring.
Lonicera nitida (Box-leaf honeysuckle) E AGR30cm (1ft) TT spring
    and summer as necessary. Dense and bushy with masses of tiny,
    box-like leaves. *L. n.* 'Baggesen's Gold' has golden leaves
    in summer.
Phillyrea angustifolia E AGR30cm (1ft) TT August. Popular in
    England during the reigns of Henry VIII and Elizabeth I, this
    eventually forms a good, thick hedge. It will need protection in
    cold, exposed sites.
Thuja plicata (Western red cedar) E AGR45cm (1ft 6in) TT late
    spring. Fast growing conifer with shiny scented foliage.

More interesting shapes

A hedge need not be cut uniformly at the same height down its entire length. They can be cut into gentle waves or even battlements. The tops of hedges can be interrupted with the occasional shape, like that of a bird or ball that can be clipped into shape from a single shoot.

STILT HEDGES

These are tall, normally straight hedges that look like square lollipops joined together on the top of bare trunks. When planted in two parallel rows they make interesting small avenues allowing views of other parts of the garden between the trunks. Hornbeam (*Carpinus betulus*)

❀ MARCH

is usually used for stilt hedges. Hardy lime (*Tilia*) can be used to produce a similar effect called 'pleaching'. This is when trees are trained onto a framework of bamboo or wire but into a narrower shape.

TAPESTRY HEDGES

Several different hedging plants can be planted together to make what is known as a 'tapestry' hedge. All sorts of plant mixtures can be used. Purple beech, yew and a golden variegated holly would eventually form a most interesting 'tapestry'.

CRINKLE-CRANKLE HEDGE

This is the word given to a wavy or serpentine hedge (or wall). The best example I can think of is at Chatsworth House in Derbyshire where a double crinkle-crankle in beech forms a vista, bordering a wide grass path leading on to a central pond at the far end.

PRICKLY CUSTOMERS

It is indeed a sad reflection on society that certain gardening books these days include in their index 'Vandal-proof plants'. I too include here a list of plants with ferocious spines to deter even the most ardent uninvited guest. It is worth noting that as I write in 1997 there is no law saying that a hedge has to be kept cut at a certain height, although walls or fences cannot exceed 2m (6ft) unless planning permission is sought. This means that anyone can allow a prickly hedge to grow to any height they want.

However, apart from their deterrent qualities, many are highly ornamental and therefore welcome additions to the garden. (Remember that prickly plants should be fenced off from young children.) Here are some suggestions for prickly hedging:

E = Evergreen D = Deciduous H = eventual Height
S = eventual Spread

Berberis julianae (Barberry) E 3m x 3m (10ft x 10ft). A dense shrub

MARCH ❁

and one of the most viciously spined of all the barberries, with spine-toothed leaves as well, copper-tinted when young. Yellow flowers in spring.

Colletia hystrix syn. *armata* D H2.5m (8ft) S2m (6ft). Almost leafless shrub covered in thick, needle-like thorns and an abundance of small, white, scented, pitcher-shaped flowers in late summer.

Pyracantha 'Orange Glow' (Firethorn) E 3m x 3m (10ft x 10ft). A vigorous, dense shrub, with orange/red berries in autumn that last well into winter.

Rosa eglanteria (Sweet briar; Eglantine rose) D 2.5 x 2.5m (8 x 8ft). Aromatic leaves and beautiful, pink, fragrant flowers followed by oval, red hips that last well into winter. Excellent for a lax hedge *R. roxburghii* (Burr rose) with shell pink flowers followed by orange-yellow hips covered in prickles.

Rubus thibetanicus (Ornamental bramble) E H2m (6ft). Purple stems with a white bloom, pretty fern-like leaves and good fruits. If you have the space, vigorous *R*. Himalaya Giant will form an impenetrable barrier and produce prolific large fruits. Also *R. cockburnianus*.

Ulex europeus 'Flore Pleno' (Gorse) D 2 x 2m (6 x 6ft) Brilliant display of yellow flowers in spring. Very useful for patches of poor ground and dry banks.

The right height

A sensible height for a hedge from the maintenance point of view is 2m (6ft). Do not cut vertically growing shoots on young hedging plants until the desired height has been attained. However, newly planted deciduous hedging plants are best reduced by one-third in height immediately after planting to reduce wind rock and to promote bushiness.

LOW-GROWING, ORNAMENTAL HEDGING PLANTS

These are plants that can be used as low hedges, about 60cm (2ft) in height, to edge different parts of the garden like paths, beds or borders. Plants should be positioned about 20cm (8in) apart.

Buxus sempervirens 'Suffruticosa' (Dwarf box) E AGR10cm (4in)
  TT August, ST. Used mostly as edging in parterres and potagers.
  Also variegated forms.
Lavandula angustifolia 'Hidcote' (Lavender) E AGR15cm (6in) TT as
  soon as the flowers begin to fade. A very effective, neatly shaped
  edging plant for a path, edge of a terrace, or as a surround for
  rose beds.
Santolina chamaecyparissus (Cotton lavender) E. AGR15cm (6in)
  TT spring and summer to remove flower heads that spoil the shape
  of the plant. Feathery, silver, aromatic foliage.
Teucrium chamaedrys (Germander) E AGR15cm (6in) TT as necessary
  in summer to maintain shape. Small pink flowers in mid summer.

Country hedges

It is a crying shame that so many country hedges have been uprooted in the name of 'efficient, modern farming methods'. Not only are we losing the hedges but the wild life that lives in them as well. We can all help to redress the balance by planting hedges consisting of countryside, as opposed to so-called 'garden', plants. Where a garden adjoins open country, that boundary should not shout out loud, but rather succeed in establishing a soft transition from one to the other. The following can be planted in a haphazard mix:

Acer campestre (Field maple)
Carpinus betulus (Hornbeam)
Crataegus monogyna (Hawthorn)
Facus sylvatica (Beech)
Hedera helix (Common English ivy)
Humulus lupulus (Hop)
Lonicera periclymenum (Common honeysuckle; Woodbine)

Rhamnus (Buckthorn)

Rosa canina (Dog rose). Any other species rose will do

Salix caprea (Pussy willow)

Sambucus nigra (Elder)

Taxus baccata (Yew)

Once the hedge is established after a few seasons, foxgloves, violets, bluebells, primroses, *Papaver rhoeas* (English poppy), wood anemones and wild strawberries can be planted at its base.

DECORATIVE SHRUBS FOR DIFFERENT SEASONS

The right choice of shrubs will give you as much year-round interest as possible. Spring and summer always bring with them a plethora of colour and scent while late summer, autumn and winter can seem far more desolate. Judicious choice will give you something to enjoy every month. All shrubs listed here have gained the Award of Garden Merit by the Royal Horticultural Society which means they are all hardy, tolerant of most soils and generally problem free. If any need special requirements I will mention them.

Here is a selection of spring-performing shrubs:

E = Evergreen S/E = Semi-Evergreen H = Height S = Spread

Berberis darwinii (Darwin's barberry) E 3.75 x 3.75m (12 x 12ft).
   Glorious display of orange-yellow flowers followed by bluish
   berries. Small, prickly, dark green leaves.
Enkianthus campanulatus 4.2 x 4.2m (14 x 14ft). Bushy, dense shrub
   with creamy-yellow flowers. Acid soils only.
Exochorda x *macrantha* 'The Bride' H2.1m (7ft) S2.4m (8ft). Dense,
   arching shrub covered in large white flowers.
Forsythia x *intermedia* 'Lynwood' 3 x 3m (10 x 10ft). The best
   of all the forsythias, with an abundance of yellow flowers. Prune

MARCH

immediately after flowering.

Magnolia stellata 3 x 3m (10 x 10ft). Masses of white starry flowers prone to frost damage.

Prunus tenella 'Fire Hill' 2 x 2m (6 x 6ft). Bushy, with masses of very deep pink flowers.

Ribes sanguineum 'Pulborough Scarlet' (Flowering currant) 7 x 7m (9 x 9ft). Covered in deep red flowers.

Rosmarinus officinalis 'Miss Jessopp's Upright' (Rosemary) E 2 x 2m (6 x 6ft). A compact, upright-growing shrub with blue flowers. Can be used as hedging.

Salix repens (Creeping willow) H60cm (2ft) S1.5m (5ft). Low growing with silky, grey catkins turning yellow.

Syringa x *persica* (Persian lilac) 2 x 2m (6 x 6ft). A bushy, dense shrub with scented purple flowers.

Here is a selection of summer-performing shrubs:

Buddleja alternifolia H3.6m (12ft) S1.8m (6ft). Arching, with grey-green leaves and masses of lilac-purple flowers hugging the stems. Can be trained as a standard.

Ceanothus impresues E H2m (6ft) S3m (10ft). One of the best of all the *ceanothus*, with masses of magnificent blue flowers. Best on a sunny wall.

Carpenteria californica E 2.1 x 2.1m (7 x 7ft). Fragrant, yellow-centred, white flowers. Needs the protection of a warm wall.

Kolkwitzia amabilis 'Pink Cloud' 3 x 3m (10 x 10ft). Masses of pink, bell-shaped flowers.

Magnolia grandiflora 'Exmouth' E. H10.5m (34ft) S9m (30ft). One of the best wall shrubs for a tall wall, with large creamy flowers. It can be grown in open ground in warmer parts of the country in protected gardens.

Myrtus communis (Common myrtle) E 3 x 3m (10 x 10ft). Aromatic dark green foliage and scented white flowers.

Philadelphus 'Belle Etoile' H2.75m (9ft) S2.1m (7ft). Highly scented,

MARCH ❁

white flowers.

Viburnum plicatum 'Mariesii' H3.6 (12ft) S4.5m (15ft). Spreading, with tiered branches along which large white flowers are neatly arranged.

Viburnum rhytidophyllum E 4.5 x 4.5m (15 x 15ft). Vigorous, with long narrow leaves and creamy white flowers.

Here is a selection of late-summer-performing shrubs:

Buddleja davidii 'Peace' (Butterfly bush) 3.5 x 3.5m (12 x 12ft). Plumes of fragrant white flowers from mid summer to autumn.

Cotinus 'Grace' (Smoke bush) 4.5 x 4.5m (15 x 15ft). Deep reddish-purple foliage and purple-pink plumes in late summer. Also striking autumn tints.

Hydrangea quercifolia (Oak-leaved hydrangea) H1.5m (5ft) S2m (6ft). Mound-forming, with dark green leaves and white flower heads. Leaves turn red and purple in autumn. All hydrangeas are useful for late summer amd autumn.

Itea ilicifolia E 3 x 3m (10 x 10ft). Long greenish catkins in amongst dark green, glossy, sharply-toothed leaves.

Tamarix ramosissima 'Rubra' 3.7 x 3.7m (12 x 12ft). Arching and graceful with fluffy spikes of deep rosy-red flowers. Useful for coastal gardens.

Yucca gloriosa (Spanish dagger) E 2 x 2m (6 x 6ft). Long, pointed leaves and pinnacles of bell-shaped white flowers.

Here is a selection of autumn-performing shrubs:

Arbutus unedo (Strawberry tree) E 6 x 6m (20 x 20ft). A large shrub/small tree with white flowers and strawberry-like flowers at the same time.

Callicarpa bodinieri var. *giraldii* 'Profusion' 2.5 x 2.5m (8 x 8ft). Bunches of decorative violet berries.

Clerodendrum trichototum 3 x 3m (10 x 10ft). Scented white flowers

❀ MARCH

followed by decorative blue berries.

Euonymus alatus (Winged spindle) H2m (6ft) S3m (10ft). Brilliant red
autumn tints with red and purple berries.

Fatsia japonica E 3 x 3m (10 x 10ft). Large, deeply lobed, dark green
leaves and dense clusters of white flowers.

Fothergilla major 2.5 x 2.5m (8 x 8ft). One of the best of all shrubs
for dazzling autumn tints, but for acid soils only.

Fremontodendron 'California Glory' S/E H6m (20ft) S4.5m (15ft).
Bright yellow flowers from late spring to mid-autumn. For a sunny
wall only. Starts to lose its vigour after about eight years.

Parrotia persica (Persian ironwood) 12 x 12m (30 x 30ft). Large
shrub/small tree with leaves turning yellow, orange and red-purple
in autumn.

Pyracantha 'Orange Glow' (Firethorn) E H5m (16ft) S3m (10ft).
Decorative orange berries. There are many other excellent
firethorns to choose from.

Here is a selection of winter-performing shrubs:

Chimonanthus praecox (Wintersweet) H2.5m (8ft) S3m (10ft). Strongly
scented yellow flowers with purple centres.

Corylus avellana 'Contorta' 5.5 x 5.5m (18 x 18ft). Curiously twisted
branches covered in yellow catkins in late winter.

Garrya elliptica 'James Roof' E H4.5m (15ft) S3.6m (12ft). Bushy and
dense with dark green, wavy-edged leaves with extra-long
grey-green catkins.

Hamamelis mollis 'Coombe Wood' (Witch hazel) 4.5 x 4.5m
(15 x 15ft). Fragrant, spidery, yellow flowers. For acid soils only.

Mahonia x media 'Charity' E 3.6 x 3.6m (12 x 12ft). Sculptural leaves
and spikes of yellow, scented flowers. *M.* Bucklandii is similar.

Rubus biflorus (Ornamental blackberry) 3 x 3m (10 x 10ft). Chalky
white young shoots. Edible yellow fruits in summer.

Sarcococca humilis E 75 x 75cm (2ft 6in x 2ft 6 in). Small white
highly scented flowers.

MARCH ❁

Viburnum x bodnantense 'Charles Lamont' 3 x 3m (10 x 10ft).
   Fragrant pink flowers in mild periods. Flowers larger and more weather resistant than *V. x b.* 'Dawn'.

MARCH TASKS

❀ Cut back the dead growth of hardy fuchsias down to ground level. Leave any longer and you may damage new emerging shoots.

❀ Thin climbers in the conservatory that have become too invasive.

❀ Plant bare-rooted bush and cane fruits in ground enriched with manure.

❀ March is the month for shaping overgrown wisterias. It is also the month for reducing those 'rats tails' back to within two leaf nodes that you have already reduced to six the preceding August. This keeps plants tidy and ensures a better show of flowers.

❀ Once snowdrops have finished flowering, congested clumps can be lifted, divided and replanted 'in the green' (that is, when the bulbs are still growing and therefore green, as opposed to dry and brown).

❀ Plant the first batch of gladioli at the end of the month. Staggered plantings will ensure a longer picking season.

❀ Protect emerging shoots of hostas and delphiniums from slugs with sharp grit, crushed egg shells, holly leaves left over from Christmas decorations, or slug pellets.

❀ Prune hybrid tea and floribunda roses, removing dead and diseased wood as you go. Cut back hard, reducing the plant by about two-thirds, always cutting above an outward-facing shoot.

❀ Cut back hard *Buddleja davidii* (the butterfly bush). If you leave it to grow as it pleases it grows into an enormous, untidy bush with disappointingly small flowers.

❀ Sow a patch of parsley, but be prepared to wait. It is very slow to germinate.

❀ Plant rhubarb in ground enriched with manure.

❀ Plant horseradish in an out-of-the-way spot. Once established, it is difficult to get rid of owing to its very deep root system.

❀ MARCH

❀ Plant mint in a punctured plastic bucket or black plastic flower pot with the rim at ground level. This prevents it from spreading.

❀ Place attractive stones on bare soil around the base of container-ized trees. This makes an attractive feature and also helps to reduce water evaporation.

MARCH ❀

Down to earth

APRIL

I HAVE BEEN BUSY ESTABLISHING the silver and white border, cutting out turf for the new enlarged shape. I couldn't ask for better soil in the ground underneath; it is easily workable down to 60cm (2ft), with no sign of clay at all. I am blessed. I do not have to double dig this area, although I am planting everything with plenty of well-rotted horse manure around their roots.

Finding the plants for this border is taking some time, but I am not prepared to compromise. If I cannot source the plants now I can always plant them in the autumn and fill the gaps with *Nicotiana sylvestris* and *N. langsdorfii* (the latter will give green flowers – they are permitted!) One of the first plants to go in was *Hemerocallis* 'Joan Senior', one of the most beautiful of all the day lilies, with the palest yellow flowers with just a hint of green. In the quest for a good white-flowering bergenia for the front of the border I settled for *B.* 'Beethoven' and for white roses towards the centre, *Rosa* 'Boule de Neige'.

For a climbing rose I have just planted the lovely scented 'Sombreuil'. Good old reliable *Artemesia* 'Powis Castle' has gone in as has *A. ludoviciana* 'Snow Queen', with completely different, silvery foliage. I have found a number of self-seeded feverfew plants and these I have planted in swathes towards the back of the border, while the white perennial pansy, *Viola cornuta* 'Alba' and the compact white-flowering cranesbill, *Geranium sanguineum* 'Album', at the front. Soon to go in is a group of twelve white gladioli and a few *Lilium regale*. Most of the cotton lavenders have flowers of too strong a yellow. *S.* 'Edward Bowles' does not, so he has been included.

POISONOUS PLANTS

I have also included an iris called 'White City'. I see that on the label is written 'Harmful if Eaten'. Well now, I didn't buy this plant in order to eat it, but I shall certainly keep this warning in mind as and when the larder is looking bare.

Foxgloves, laburnums and bluebells, to mention just three of a very long list, are often referred to as poisonous, as a warning, I presume, for parents of toddlers. The President of the RHS suggested recently that such plants should be labelled as 'Potentially Harmful'. This is less alarmist, although I would imagine munching your way through the herbaceous border would give you a very nasty tummy pain, but luckily most of us have the common sense not to do so. I have known anxious parents to cut down an old and beautiful laburnum because of these warnings, a needless over-reaction resulting in unnecessary destruction.

A SPLASH OF YELLOW

One of the most exciting new climbers to have appeared in recent years is the yellow form of the common jasmine, *Jasminum officinale* 'Fiona Sunrise'. Its flowers are just as strongly scented as common jasmine, which is so useful for covering tall north-facing house walls, but what is very special about it is its yellow foliage. Up until 1995, when Hilliers Nurseries launched it at the Chelsea Flower Show, there were only two other good climbers with striking yellow foliage, the perennial yellow-leaved hop, *Humulus lupulus* 'Aureus' and the ivy *Hedera helix* 'Buttercup'. Found as a chance seedling in a batch of

APRIL

seeds sent from the Himalayan area of north India, this yellow-leaved jasmine was grown on and remained true to colour and its potential as a wonderful new garden plant was immediately recognized. It is this plant I have chosen to climb over my new dark green, plastic, 'slimline', state-of-the-art oil tank underneath the dovecote. I planted it yesterday.

GOOD SPORTS

Choisya ternata 'Sundance', the yellow-leaved version of Mexican Orange Blossom was also found by chance in similar circumstances. It is not a plant I would readily entertain in my garden as I find the leaf too acid a yellow, although if grown in the shade the acidity mellows to a more agreeable clear yellow. My reason for mentioning both these plants is because they have become enormously popular, but would never have been brought to the public's attention had an experienced plantsman not noticed them as 'sports' (shoots that are different from all the others on the same plant) in the beginning. I wonder how many potentially commercial plants have been lost to horticulture merely because they belonged to an amateur gardener who never recognized their value?

WHERE IS THE SPRING?

This is going to be a very late season indeed. Uncharacteristically cold weather has resulted in daffodils being a long way from flowering and there is little sign of bud-break on trees and shrubs. I am still busy planting shrubs at the front of the house although local nursery stocks are thin on the ground as they have not yet dared buy in new stock. I am having to leave gaps for plants when I manage to acquire them.

I have made my first sowing of rocket, under cloches, as the ground is still so cold and wet.

Where is the spring I wonder ?

APRIL

HOLLIES

Where the apples march down the now wattle-fence-screened south side of the large garden, I am planning to plant a vegetative screen to replace the wattle when it eventually collapses in 30 years time or so, in order to screen off the neighbouring houses. This screen will be largely of hollies, of which there exist a great many (180 are listed in *The Plant Finder,* 1996 edition). A few years ago I walked around the Savill Gardens at Great Windsor Park with John Bond, the curator, and he opened my eyes to the virtues of the *ilex* (holly) genus.

The first thing to remember about hollies is that they are either berry-producing females or non berry-producing males, although there do exist a very few hermaphrodites, with male and female organs on the same plant, the most well known being *I. aquifolium* 'J.C. van Tol', good for a small garden. If there is a good crop of berries, it means that there were favourable conditions for cross-pollination the preceding spring. One male close by every three or four females should do the trick. I will need to protect all these hollies from rabbits, who find them a delicacy, especially when young.

Hollies are rarely planted because they have the reputation of being slow-growing. This is not the case with the vigorous and tree-like male Highclere hollies like 'Jermyns' and 'Hodginsii', the female x *altaclerensis* species like 'Purple Shaft', 'Golden King' and 'Silver Sentinel' which can grow to 50ft or more. Varieties of this species include 'Hendersonii', female with brown/red berries and 'Jermyns', male, almost spineless with green stems. Other tall growers include *Ilex dipyrena*, female with dark red berries and *I. macrocarpa*, a deciduous female with large black berries the size of small cherries. I will plant some hedgehog hollies (*I. aquifolium* 'Ferox' and varieties) – they are all male – towards the front of the screen, for their fascinating twisted leaves covered in spines on both sides. I have been preparing holes for the hollies for planting this autumn.

NEVER TOO YOUNG TO START

The best thing that ever happened to me was being given a garden of my own when I was a child. All children should have their own plot, even if it is a single pot on a balcony, but to encourage them with success they must be given a sunny spot with good soil. Children are impatient by nature and should be given fast-growing plants like giant sunflowers, love-in-a-mist, Iceland poppies, nasturtiums and marigolds, which are all colourful as well. I haven't yet decided exactly where Alexandra's, Natasha's and Rosie's gardens are going to go.

POTTERING ABOUT

For a greenhouse I have roofed in a strangely shaped outhouse with clear corrugated PVC and built wooden staging. My hand-turned terracotta pots, which I have been collecting over the years, look wonderful even when sitting there empty, especially my Long Toms destined to grow red cherry tomatoes this year, although Uncle Tony (who is now, sadly, dead) always swore that yellow tomatoes were tastier than red varieties. I spend many happy hours in my new retreat potting and pottering about.

PLANTS FOR DISGUISE

Oil and gas tanks and dustbins rank top of the list when it comes to eyesores and it is especially important to disguise them in small gardens where it is difficult to tuck them away out of sight. There are ways of making them into decorative features.

Dustbins

Dustbins can have a square bunker built for them in stone, breeze block or brick with an alpine trough as a roof and a simple wooden

APRIL

door on one side. The trough on top need only be 15cm (6in) deep at most, made of hardwood, lined on the inside with thin PVC sheeting to protect the wood. Puncture the liner here and there to allow for drainage and fill it with a quick-draining compost. Alpines can then be planted with special stones dotted amongst them and then a final fine gravel mulch spread over the compost. Pave inside the bunker so that the bin can be pushed in and pulled out easily. If breeze blocks are used they should be painted in dark green or another colour of your choice.

A quicker, easier and cheaper alternative is to build a square trellis surround with a trellis roof, supported on posts at each corner. On the convenient side the trellis panel should be hinged to act as a door. A whole variety of climbers can be trained up and over the trellis including one of the large-leaved ivies like *Hedera canariensis* 'Gloire de Marengo', honeysuckle (especially *Lonicera periclymenum* 'Belgica'), *Actinidia kolomikta* with white and pink-variegated leaves, or Passion Flower (*Passiflora caerulea*).

Oil and gas tanks

The more modern state-of-the-art PVC oil tanks are an improvement on the old square ones that always went rusty after a time, but they are nonetheless oil tanks! Climber-clad trellis screens are certainly one solution although they could also be disguised as a good-looking roofed cupboard, with handsome doors, perhaps with moulding, either painted or stained a discreet colour. If space allows, a larger cupboard could be built to accommodate tool storage, so killing two birds with one stone. Self-clinging climbers like any of the ivies, e.g., evergreen *Hedera helix* 'Gold Heart' with white-variegated leaves, or deciduous Virginia creeper (*Parthenocissus tricuspidata* 'Veitchii') can be allowed to scramble over a tank at will.

With a little imagination, even the most ghastly eyesore in the garden can be turned into an attractive feature – perhaps even a vista-stopper – at no great cost.

APRIL ❀

PLANTS FOR CHILDREN

Children are impatient by nature and only enjoy growing plants that grow exceptionally fast on an open, sunny patch of good soil in ground already prepared, where success is more likely to result in a love of gardening for life. The best fast-growing plants for children to start off with are:

Flowers

Sunflowers; choose single-flowered, giant varieties for the most
    spectacular results. A few seeds can be kept for the following
    season and the rest can be fed to the birds.
Nasturtiums can be encouraged to scramble up hedges over shrubs
    Their flowers are very colourful and can be used, along with
    the leaves, in salads.
Marigolds are very colourful and very easy to grow.
Sweet peas; their scent will remain a special childhood memory.
Cornflowers are quick to germinate and are very colourful.
Love-in-a-mist has very pretty flowers and good seed heads.
Snapdragons; squeeze the flowers on the sides and watch their
    mouths open.

Vegetables

Children take great pride in producing food for the table. It makes eating food that is good for you fun:

Runner beans have bright and colourful red flowers.
Radishes crop very quickly.
Courgettes, pumpkins, squashes and ornamental gourds all grow fast
    and give quick rewards. There's nothing like having grown your
    own pumpkin for Halloween and ornamental gourds can be used
    for winter decoration in the house.

APRIL

Lettuce germinates very fast and can be cropped a few weeks after planting out.

Tomatoes. Try an ornamental variety like 'Tigerella' with skins striped in red and yellow, cherry tomatoes or a good old reliable like 'Red Alert'.

Peas: what is more delicious than eating peas straight from the pod?

GREAT OAKS FROM LITTLE ACORNS GROW

Conkers (horse chestnut), walnuts and acorns (oak) are amongst the easiest tree seeds to grow. The problem is that they will not be happy left growing in their pots for longer than a couple of seasons, and because they eventually grow into enormous trees, they should not be planted in small gardens whatever their sentimental value!

APRIL

Plants to grow for children

To give children pleasure in the garden, grow as many plants as you can to attract butterflies, especially *Buddleja davidii* for swarms of butterflies in late summer. Chinese lanterns (*Physalis*) bear fascinating orange lanterns in late summer and autumn that can be picked and used as decoration indoors in winter. In the greenhouse, the Venus Flytrap is always good value. The macabre spectacle of watching flies being trapped in the hairy jaws of this plant is as good as a science fiction triffid any day. The Sensitive Plant will also fascinate children. Gently stroke the leaves; not only will the individual leaves close up tight but the whole plant bows down as well. Finally, cacti are always popular with children, especially when they flower.

Children's water features

The easiest way of building a little pond is to dig a small hole, line it with a black dustbin liner and disguise the edge with stones and shells. This makes an excellent centrepiece for colourful planting, with a little path leading up to it.

Children have a fascination with water, especially when it comes to watching wildlife. A small pond will attract frogs (and with any luck tadpoles), newts, water boatmen and dragonflies. Water-loving plants, water snails and fish can also be introduced (see wildlife ponds, page 140).

A child-safe pond

A young child can drown in a mere few inches of water. There is a way of safeguarding against this by filling a small pond with stones and pebbles. This does not preclude you from being able to have marginal aquatics and a fountain. Once the children are older, the stones can be removed and fish can take their place.

Trees for children

Trees always prove a great source of fascination for children, especially if they have been planted to mark a special occasion such as the child's own birth. This teaches them, from a very young age, how fast a tree grows — compared to a child.

TEACHING CHILDREN THE DANGERS

If children are discouraged from eating plants they are less likely to do so. However, the twos and threes are dangerous ages when children experiment and seldom take in what you are saying. If, for instance, you have a laburnum growing in your garden, it should be fenced off until they are old enough not to be tempted to pick up and eat the fallen seeds.

There are a number of plants with particularly toxic properties and these include:

APRIL

* = all parts are poisonous

* *Aconitum* (Monkshood or Wolf's bane). Can cause fatal poisoning.
* *Aesculus* (Horsechestnut). Conkers are the worst threat.
Alstroemeria. Skin irritation can develop if the leaves are
   handled continuously.
* *Aquilegia* (Columbine or Granny's bonnets).
* Arum lily.
* *Colchicum.* Highly toxic.
Convallaria (Lily-of-the-valley). Poisonous seeds.
Daphne mezereum. Toxic berries.
* *Datura* (Angel's trumpets).
* Delphinium.
* *Digitalis* (Foxglove).
Heracleum (Giant hogweed). Can cause a nasty skin irritation.
* *Euonymus.* Berries the worst threat.
* *Euphorbia* (Spurge). Milky sap may cause skin irritation.
Fremontodendron. Hairy stems may cause skin irritation.
* *Hedera* (Ivy).
* *Helleborus* (Christmas rose).
Ipomea (Morning glory). Toxic seeds.
* *Hyacinthoides* (Hyacinth and bluebells).
* Laburnum.
* *Lupinus* (Lupin). Seeds.
Narcissus (Daffodil). Especially bulbs.
Primula. Especially varieties of *P. obconica*.
Prunus laurocerasus (Cherry laurel). Berries.
Ruta (Rue). Especially the leaves in bright sunlight.
Solanum tuberosum (Potatoes). All green parts are poisonous.
Taxus baccata (Yew). The fleshy red seed capsule tastes quite nice – it
   is the small black seed inside that is highly toxic.
Wisteria. Toxic seeds.

PONDS AND OTHER WATER FEATURES

I have often wondered why water is so fascinating to man. Is it because our very distant ancestors used to live in it? No one can deny that moving water in a garden is a positive delight. Apart from its mystique it also supplies music and attracts wildlife. Every garden, however small, even a balcony, should include a water feature of some sort.

Noise pollution

Water is a positive advantage for people living in urban areas or close to a busy road. The musical trickling of water magically succeeds in muffling the drone of traffic.

Submersible pumps

No one has to rely any more on a natural source of water to include moving water in a garden. The advent of the submersible pump has changed all that. This is a pump that sits under the water and recycles the same water from a pond to a fountain head or cascade and back again. Submersible pumps come in different sizes depending on how much water needs to be shifted, how far and to what height. Pumps should be installed by a qualified electrician and attached to a circuit breaker in case of accidental damage.

Small water features

The smallest water feature I have ever seen consisted of a plastic bucket sunk into the ground. In it sat a submersible pump that propelled a small fountain. The plastic liner that filled the bucket overlapped some distance all the way round, about 1m (3ft) in diameter, so that as much water as possible percolated back into the bucket on windy days. Stones and pebbles were arranged on a perforated lid

APRIL

over the bucket and the surrounding liner to make it look like a stony outcrop. The electric cable leading back to the house was laid under the liner.

> TIP: HANDY SWITCHES
>
> To prevent you from having to go outside to turn on your fountain, position the switch somewhere indoors, by the door leading out into the garden or by a window that commands a view of it.

FOR A BALCONY

A wooden half-barrel makes an ideal water feature for a balcony. As an extra precaution against leaks the inside of the barrel can be lined with a plastic liner, trimmed neatly at the edge. You can include a small fountain within the barrel, or have the water feeding it via a wall-mounted mask. A variety of small aquatic plants as well as fish and wildlife like snails can then be entertained.

Small informal ponds

The first thing to get right is the actual position of your proposed pond. A semi-shaded spot is preferable in order to reduce the clouding of the water by algae, resulting in a pea soup effect. This shading is best supplied by evergreen plants, walls or fences as decidous trees drop leaves into the water which in turn go black and slimy and clog pump filters.

ALGAE

The formation of algae in water which turns it an unsightly green colour is most pond owners' bugbear. There are ways of reducing it. The sunnier the pond, the worse the algae problem tends to be, so apart from siting the pond in the shade, the water itself can be shaded by water-loving plants, especially water lilies. A fountain also helps to

APRIL

keep water clear because water kept on the move is constantly being oxygenated. However, some ponds remain obstinately algae-ridden despite every attempt to remedy them.

SEMI-RIGID LINERS

One of the simplest and easiest types of small pond to install is an off-the-shelf semi-rigid liner sunk into the ground into a hole about 15cm (6in) deeper and wider than the module. It should be cushioned on a bed of sand or turf and, when being filled, sand should be added around the sides, keeping to the same level as the water to prevent stress to the superstructure. The only problem with semi-rigid liners is that the shape is already decided for you, so if you want to design your own pond, you will need to line it with a flexible liner.

FLEXIBLE LINERS

Flexible liners are the best answer for larger ponds. They are sold in varying thicknesses at comprehensive garden centres and specialist aquatic centres, the thicker ones being the more expensive. They come in strips of about 1m (3ft) wide which can be heat-sealed together if necessary. So long as the pond is cushioned with sand it should not be necessary to install the thickest liner, but I always err on the side of caution, dig deep in my pocket and use the most expensive.

When using flexible liners, it is important to remove anything sharp which could puncture the liner, but also anything organic like turf, pieces of wood or old roots, to prevent methane gas from building up under the liner (see page 63).

DISGUISING THE EDGE

The main fault of flexible liners is that they crease and look unsightly towards the edge of ponds. Algae will discolour these creases in time although stones laid slightly overlapping the edge will help in the short term. In the case of wildlife ponds, swathes of turf or round pebbles can be laid over the edge and down into the water.

APRIL

LEVEL EDGES

It is vital to ensure that the edges all the way round the pond are level. When you come to fill the pond you do not want to find that the water starts pouring out on one side when it hasn't yet reached the top on the other.

Formal ponds

Square, rectangular and hexagonal ponds and formal canals are features for more formal gardens. They need to be built by specialists and not by ordinary builders. Unfortunately, I do not have the space here to do justice to the subject, but for further reading I can recommend *The Water Gardener* by Anthony Archer-Wills, published by Frances Lincoln.

Encouraging wildlife

If you have water in the garden you will always have wildlife. This will add enormous interest to the garden and is also educational for children.

A wildlife pond is easily built using a flexible liner with the edge covered in upside down turf, earth or stones. The water depth should vary from 45cm (18in) to 1m (3ft) and the sides should slope gently. The main ingredients for a wildlife pond are:

❀ The occasional large stone for birds to clean their beaks on and for small amphibians to rest and sunbathe on.
❀ Nooks and crannies between large stones supply cool places for amphibians in summer.
❀ Sunny and shaded areas.
❀ Duckweed, a favourite food of ducks.
❀ Cover by the water's edge like reeds, rushes and iris for shy birds. Also native trees like elder and hawthorn.
❀ Oxygenating plants to help keep the water clean.

1   LEVELLING THE EDGES OF A POND

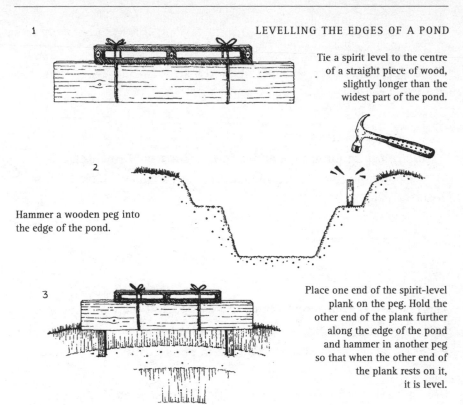

Tie a spirit level to the centre
of a straight piece of wood,
slightly longer than the
widest part of the pond.

2

Hammer a wooden peg into
the edge of the pond.

3

Place one end of the spirit-level
plank on the peg. Hold the
other end of the plank further
along the edge of the pond
and hammer in another peg
so that when the other end of
the plank rests on it,
it is level.

4

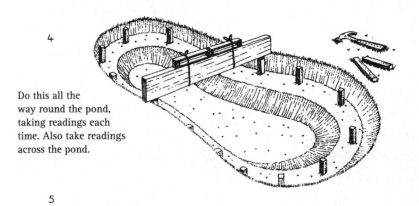

Do this all the
way round the pond,
taking readings each
time. Also take readings
across the pond.

5

You will now have a
level row of pegs all around
the pond. Dig away excess soil
so that the lip of the
pond is level.

❖ APRIL

❀ A pebble beach to provide a gentle slope for feeding mammals and bathing birds.
❀ Native, water-loving plants like loosestrife, meadowsweet and Joe Pye Weed to attract indigenous fauna.

TIP: ANIMAL SAFETY

❀ To prevent domestic and wild animals from drowning in a pond, place a small wooden ramp at its edge for easy escape.

Water-loving plants

There are several different kinds of water-loving plants. Some like to have their roots sitting at the bottom of a pond, some float on the water surface and others like growing in permanently wet ground.

Here is a selection of hardy perennials for wet soils edging ponds:

H = Height S = Spread

Aruncus dioicus (Goat's beard) H1.5-1.8m (5-6ft) S1m (3ft). Beautiful fern-like leaves, bronze when young, and large plumes of creamy flowers.

Astilbe 'Venus' 1 x 1m (3 x 3ft). Plumes of shell-pink flowers useful as winter decoration.

Carex elata 'Aurea'. Also called *Carex stricta* 'Bowles' Golden' (Bowles' golden sedge).

Gunnera manicata 2-3 x 2-3m (6-10 x 6-10ft). Huge leaves up to 1.5m (5ft) across and conical rusty seed heads. Protect the crown in winter by placing the dying leaves upside down over the plant.

Hemerocallis fulva 'Flore Pleno' (Day Lily) H1-1.2m (3-4ft) S75cm (2ft 6in). Handsome strap-like leaves and orange-buff, trumpet-shaped, double flowers.

Hosta 'Frances Williams' (Plantain lily) H1m (3ft) S1.5m (5ft). Large,
 heart-shaped, glaucous blue leaves with creamy margin and
 lavender blue flowers. All hostas love damp soils.

Osmunda regalis (Royal fern) H2m (6ft) S1m (3ft). Elegant fern and
 pale brown flower spikes.

Rheum palmatum Atrosanguineum (Ornamental rhubarb). Large
 ornamental leaves and spikes of rust-red flowers in early summer.

Primula pulverulenta (Candelabra primula) H60cm (2ft) S30-45cm
 (1-1·5ft). Beautiful red tubular flowers. Most primulas prefer moist
 conditions.

Rodgersia podophylla H1.2m (4ft) S1m (3ft). Large attractive leaves
 and cream flowers.

Here is a selection of hardy perennial marginal plants that like growing in shallow water on a pond's edge:

Acorus calamus 'Variegatus' (Myrtle flag, Sweet flag) H75cm (2.5ft)
 S 60cm (2ft). Grown for its cream-striped, iris-like leaves.

Eriphorum augustifolium (Common cotton grass) H30-45cm
 (12-18in) S indefinite. Evergreen, dense tufts of grass-like leaves
 and white fluffy 'cotton balls'.

Iris versicolor (Blue flag, Wild iris) H60cm (2ft) S indefinite. Beautiful
 violet-blue flowers.

Lysichiton americanus (Yellow skunk cabbage) H1.2m (4ft) S75cm
 (2.5ft). Wonderful yellow arum-like spathes in spring followed by
 large leaves. *L. camtschatcensis* has white spathes.

Orontium aquaticum (Golden club) H30-45cm (12-18in) S60cm
 (2ft). Poker-like, yellow-tipped flower heads and bluish-green
 leaves.

Phragmites australis 'Variegatus'. Very invasive reed grass with leaves
 striped with bright yellow and heads of purple flowers

❖ APRIL

Hardy water lilies need plenty of sun in still, or almost still, water.
They are planted in perforated baskets available at garden centres and

specialist aquatic centres. Young plants are best started off close to the water surface sitting on bricks and, as the plants gain strength, the bricks are moved one at a time until the plant sits on the bottom of the pond. Plants need thinning when leaves become over-congested (when they stick up out of the water as opposed to lying flat on the water surface and few flowers are produced).

There are many varieties to choose from, some preferring shallow and some deep, water, with flowers ranging from orange and yellow to white, pink and red. Their leaves provide valuable shade to help to keep water clear.

Here is a selection of hardy water lilies (*nymphaea*):

WD = Water depth   S = Spread

Nymphaea alba (Common white water lily) WD30-90cm (1-3ft) S1.5-2m (5-6ft). A prolific flowerer suited to a large pond. Each flower is 20cm (8in) across and is magnolia-white with yellow stamens.

N. 'Froebelii' WD15-30cm (6in-1ft) S1m (3ft). Deep red flowers with orange red stamens.

N. 'Gonnere' WD30-45cm (12-18in) S1-1.2m (3-4ft). Beautiful, double, scented white flowers.

N. 'Pink Sensation' WD30-45cm (12-18in) S1.2m (4ft). Pink flowers and yellow stamens.

N. 'William Falconer' WD45-75cm (18-30in) S1.2m (4ft). Gorgeous, deep red flowers and yellow stamens.

N. tetragona 'Alba' WD15-22cm (6-9in) S60-90cm (2-3ft). Ideal for shallower water, with white flowers.

Submerged plants take root in either soil placed at the bottom of a pond or in baskets. They are also known as 'oxygenators' as they help to maintain clear water. Their roots absorb nutrients from fish waste. They tend to be very invasive and should be thinned regularly.

Here is a selection of submerged plants:

Ceratophyllum demersum (Hornwort) WD60cm (2ft) or deeper,
   S indefinite. Slender stems and forked leaves. Tolerant of shade.
Hottonia palustris (Water violet) WD to 45cm (18in) S indefinite.
   Height of pale lilac flowers 30-90cm (1-3ft).
Lagarosiphon major (also called *Elodea crispa*) WD1m (3ft)
   S indefinite. Forms a dense mass of branching stems on the water
   surface as well as below the water.
Ranunculus aquatilis (Water crowfoot) WD up to 1m (3ft) S indefinite.
   Ideal for a wildlife pond where it can root in wet mud. White
   flowers with yellow centres just above the water surface.

WARNING

❀ Common duckweed (*Lemna minor*) is very invasive and can
become a real nuisance in large ponds. Each plant consists
of a tiny pale green floating frond with a small root and
eventually forms a carpet over the whole pond. Normally
introduced into ponds on the feet of visiting birds, it can be
kept under control by removing it with a net.

APRIL

APRIL TASKS

❀ Repot cacti in loam-based compost mixed with plenty of grit to
ensure good drainage. Use a collar of paper or sponge for protection.
❀ Pinch out the leading shoot on sweet peas to encourage more side
shoots and therefore more flowers.
❀ A hoe on a dry day now will save you a lot of extra work later
when the weeds have grown large.
❀ Position supports for herbaceous perennials. These can be of dead
twiggy material or specially made meshed hoops on legs.
❀ Tidy up the rockery. Remove plants that have overgrown their
alloted space and replace them with something new.

❀ When sowing very fine seed, water the compost in seed trays first, otherwise the seed can be washed deep into the compost.

❀ When pricking out seedlings, always handle them by the leaf and not the stem to avoid damaging them.

❀ Keep a watering can full of water in a warm room to take the chill out of the water destined for seedlings.

❀ Install more water butts fed by down-pipes from gutters to make sure you have adequate water in case of a dry summer.

❀ 'Layer' most shrubs this month. Choose a branch that is easily bent down to the ground. Where it touches the soil, nick it with a sharp knife and peg it to the ground so that the wound is under the soil surface. Roots will form from this wound. Keep it well watered in dry spells in summer and by the autumn the rooted shoot can be severed from the parent plant and planted out on its own.

❀ Plant onion sets 15cm (6in) apart, barely covering them. This is a much quicker way of growing onions than sowing them from seed.

❀ Replace plant labels whose writing has become faint, repositioning them where they are easily read.

❀ Unpack mail order plants the minute they are delivered. Wet their roots and plant them without delay. Frost-tender plants will need to be kept in the greenhouse for a while yet.

❀ Prepare holes for dahlias. They like it rich, so incorporate generous amounts of well-rotted organic matter as well as a sprinkling of slow-release fertilizer such as Osmocote or fish, blood and bone.

❀ Prune out dead and damaged wood on ornamental trees.

❀ Prune hard back dogwoods and willows grown for winter colour.

❀ Whitewash greenhouse glass. This diffuses the sun's rays and keeps the greenhouse cooler. Also keep ventilators open on sunny days.

❀ Make the first sowing of rocket, surely the tastiest of all the salad crops. Sow every month for continual supply.

❀ Surplus seed should be kept for next year in an airtight tin kept in a cool place.

❀ Treat wooden posts, fences and garden furniture with a preservative on a dry day.

A busy month in the garden

MAY

THERE ARE SO MANY GARDEN GADGETS on the market these days that it numbs the mind. As the gardening correspondent for the *Mail on Sunday*, I am constantly being sent press releases for them, especially for lawn mowers, each promising to be more exciting and technologically revolutionary than the last. Well, I may be a bit of a Luddite but it seems to me they have become needlessly complicated and less efficient. The endless technological development has resulted in a breed of mowers nearly as complicated as my computer (which, I am afraid, I still haven't mastered). Now made in lightweight this and that, presumably designed for the willowy, bikini-clad models who promote them in brochures, they almost feel too light to be of any use. I yearn for the trusty old Atco mower of my youth - its very weight and solidity inspired confidence. I do see the sense of lightweight machines for mowing steep banks, but give me a solid, weighty machine every time for my flat lawn.

Having said that, I have recently invested in a mechanized wheelbarrow. Like all things well-designed it is the easiest machine to operate, having only one control, the accelerator, positioned just underneath the handle on the right. It has proved enormously helpful to me, as I am sure other gadgets are to other people — only if you collected them all, there'd be room for nothing else in your garden.

WAR WEEDING

Talk of lawn mowers reminds me of my grandparents' (my mother's parents) home at Shrubland Hall in Suffolk, one of the family houses owned by my grandfather, Lord de Saumarez. During World War II, what with petrol being unavailable and the gardeners away fighting for King and Country, the lawns were mown by contraptions pulled by Suffolk Punch horses with their feet wrapped in special leather shoes to protect the turf. My mother, who was a lorry driver for the WRNS, based at Portsmouth during the war, was always made to do an hour's weeding before breakfast by my grandmother whenever she took leave there.

PLANT FOODS

Another thing seemingly designed to confuse is the vast array of plant foods available today. I have whittled them down to a few. For trees, shrubs and perennials I use a slow-release fertilizer, such as Osmocote granules. They only release nutrients to plants when growing conditions are right (when the ground is warm enough). If planting in the spring or autumn I sprinkle them around the roots before I 'piddle' them in, or else I sprinkle them around the base of established plants in February and lightly work them into the soil with a hand fork. (To 'piddle' is horticultural jargon for soaking the hole at planting time.)

I continue to use those other two famous slow-release fertilizers, bonemeal and fish, blood and bone. I use them on ornamental trees and shrubs as I am confident that they cannot find their way into the food chain but, because of the risk, however slight, of BSE, I would be reluctant to use them on vegetables and fruit or any other crop destined for the table.

For a 'quick fix', I use the seaweed-based Maxicrop, every two weeks or so, or whenever I can remember. It has roughly the same effect as you or I drinking a glass of whisky. Applied with a rose on a watering can, the nutrients quickly find their way into the very core of the plant via the roots *and* the leaves. It is often forgotten that plants absorb nutrients (and water) via the leaves. In the same vein, young evergreen conifers should always have their foliage soaked when being watered, especially during protracted dry spells.

A DRY START

It continues to be a very dry start to the season. I have lost nothing in the winter, despite the fact that I was busy planting between blizzards, but then I did give them all a good mulch which helps to protect shallow root systems from the cold. Even my Loquat (*Eriobotrya japonica*) is producing a great rosette of new leaves. It is a pity that this plant is seldom seen for sale. I cannot understand why as it makes a truly handsome plant for a sunny wall or fence and is remarkably hardy considering its exotic name and looks. I do not mind that it is unlikely to fruit in my cold, exposed garden despite the fact that it is planted at the base of a south-facing wall. I am quite happy just admiring its foliage which is not dissimilar to that of *Magnolia grandiflora* – anyway at a distance.

The elder is just beginning to blossom and I look forward to a bit more seasonal warmth in order to be able to enjoy the wonderfully refreshing elderflower cordial my wife, Tania, makes from the elderflowers (see the recipe on page 150).

May is always a busy month in the garden as everything is growing so fast. The first cut of the spring cabbage soon followed a first sowing of rocket in April and I have started to stake herbaceous perennials, things that should have been done weeks ago, but the season is still a month late. Against my instincts I have planted out a few white cactus dahlia tubers as fillers for the silver and white border and have just repotted my Indian Azalea into a nice terracotta pot containing acid compost. I have put it up against a north-facing wall where it will be watered regularly with water from a nearby butt. It will grow well and flourish in the cool temperatures with its compost

❧ MAY

kept constantly wet. I have taken all the houseplants, the banana, the agave, the tender geraniums and so on outside for their summer holidays. We're all going to the Witterings and Scotland (no, not the plants), but not until August.

ELDERFLOWER CORDIAL

15 flower heads, picked just as the flowers have opened
4 unwaxed lemons, roughly chopped
2 kg (4½lb) granulated sugar
4 litres (8 pints) boiled water
15ml (1 tablespoon) citric acid

Put flower heads in a large plastic bucket or bowl having first removed stalks. Add lemons, sugar and citric acid and cover with the boiling water. Stir until sugar dissolves, cover with tea towel and leave for 2-3 days. Strain into bottles and keep refridgerated. Drink diluted with water (as a cordial) within two months, or freeze (in plastic bottles) for later use. Also delicious as a syrup for fresh fruit salad.

Elderflower heads can also be used as a flavour enhancer for gooseberries. When stewing gooseberries lay a few heads on the top of the fruit whilst cooking and remove before serving. They can also be fried in batter, just like courgette flowers.

ELDERFLOWER SPRITZER

For the grown-ups, use elderflower cordial to make this most refreshing of summer cocktails:

Half a tumbler of white wine
Top up with fizzy water
Add a dash of elderflower cordial
Serve on the rocks

What could be more delicious after a hard day's gardening – there is such a lot to do in the garden in May.

CONTAINER GARDENING

Plants in containers are a welcome addition to any garden. Container planting also allows you to grow exotic species that cannot survive harsh winters, as you can move them indoors or into a sheltered place when the frosts come. The containers themselves form part of the attraction as they come in so many shapes, sizes and colours. All plants will grow in practically any container, as long as it has holes in the bottom for drainage – anything from a disused boat to a car tyre, giving the gardener an inexhaustible list of possibilities. Of course, choice of container and plant is entirely personal. All I can do is to tell you of some examples of containerized plants that I have either put together myself or seen and admired, in the hope that they will inspire you.

Places for containers

There is room for a containerized plant in every garden, as I hope I can show you below. Pots are also the answer for frustrated gardeners with tiny gardens or patios – you can even grow things in containers if all you have is a balcony or window sill. Here are some of the best uses for pots:

❀ To frame a doorway
❀ To decorate a balcony or terrace
❀ To line a path or steps
❀ To fill a gap in the border
❀ To decorate a window sill
❀ To decorate a wall

Planting ideas

I have seen the most amazing things in pots, ranging from a full vegetable garden to a single giant specimen plant. With the correct care

MAY

and conditions, your imagination is the only limit to what you can grow in containers. Here are some plant 'recipes' to start you off:

FOR ADDED HEIGHT

Plant recipe: sweet peas or runner beans on a bamboo cane wigwam. Underplant with fraises des bois and ivy-leaved geraniums tumbling over the edge.

Effects: lots of colour; flowers to pick; strawberries to eat.

Best in: June-August.

Container: large wooden half-barrel, Versailles tub or any large terracotta pot.

MAY

To achieve height in a container, train climbing plants on a cane wigwam.

Position: on a terrace or patio. Full or part sun.

Care: water and feed well in hot weather.

Alternatives: a trellis pyramid using Morning Glory underplanted with *Senecio cineraria* for a rich and cool, blue and silver display.

DECORATIVE HERBS

Plant recipe: bronze fennel, or a bay clipped to a lollipop shape in the centre for height, surrounded by golden marjoram, purple sage, parsley, chives and silver thyme.

Effects: contrasting foliage; small, but pretty flowers; aromatic leaves; herbs to use in cooking. Foliage all year (all these plants are perennial except parsley and these should be thinned and replanted every two years or so).

Best in: flowers in June-August.

Container: any, but herbs look especially good in terracotta.

Position: full sun.

Care: water a little if extremely dry. Herbs like dry, hot conditions.

EDIBLE CONTAINER COLLECTIONS

Plant recipe 1: tomatoes, such as 'Gardener's Delight' (a red cherry variety); 'Tigerella' (red and orange striped skin or 'Golden Sunrise' (yellow fruits).

Effects: attractive foliage and ripening fruits; tomatoes to eat.

Best in: harvest July-August.

Container: growing bag or any pot.

Position: full sun, sheltered.

Care: tomatoes are thirsty, so water regularly. Feed with a commercial tomato food every week once the fruit start to grow.

Plant recipe 2: strawberries such as 'Cambridge Favourite' and 'Aromel'.

Effects: lush folage, small flowers, ripening fruit; delicious strawberries to harvest.

Best in: harvest June-August.

❀ MAY

Container: strawberry pot, with special planting holes, any medium-sized pot, growing bag, trough or hanging basket.
Position: full sun or part shade.
Care: water in very hot, dry periods.

Plant recipe 3: citrus fruit: oranges, lemons, grapefruit and all the other citrus are best bought as plants from specialist nurseries or garden centres. Plants grown from pips often come true (bear the same fruit as the parent plant) but they can take about five years or longer to flower and fruit.
Effects: attractive, shiny foliage; flowers and pretty fruit if the tree is mature enough.
Best in: flowers in May; fruit in July-August.
Container: any, depending on size of plant.
Position: see care, below.
Care: citrus fruit need to spend the winter under glass so, before the first frosts, plants must be moved into warmer conditions (greenhouse, conservatory or indoors). During this time citrus like as much light as possible and a temperature of not less than 4°C (40°F). A sunny window sill will do as long as it is not directly over a radiator. Once the threat of frost is over, usually about the end of May, take outside into a protected, shaded spot, to prevent leaf scorch. Gradually move your container to a sunnier position. Once it has acclimatized, leave out in the sunniest position possible for the remainder of the summer.

The best time to repot citrus is in late spring using a good, coarse, soil-less potting compost, with added bark to ensure efficient drainage.

They are greedy plants and need constant year-round feeding if they are to crop well, using a specialist feed bought from comprehensive garden centres. Foliar feeding once a week, using the same solution in winter and spring, can greatly increase fruit yield. The most important thing to remember is not to over-water citrus trees. The way to water them all year round is to give them a good soak and then not water them again until the leaves start to flag.

MAY

ABOVE A bunch of sweet peas in mid-summer is heaven-scent!

RIGHT Wood, stone, terracotta and morning glory – a heavenly quartet. This photograph was taken in my greenhouse.

ABOVE The white-painted trunk of the apricot tree – just about visible in the background – acts as a vista-stopper beyond the pond.

RIGHT The frame of what will one day be a box topiary chicken, with self-sown pansies.

LEFT Osteospermums on the new terrace outside the drawing room.

RIGHT There is little so cooling and musical as the splash of water on a hot summer's day.

RIGHT My daughter Rosie in her little garden ablaze with convolvulus.

BELOW My vegetable garden – broad beans must be so comfortable in that soft, furry pod!

Plant recipe 4: aubergines or sweet peppers.

Effects: the purple-black fruit of aubergines and the yellow, red or orange fruits of sweet peppers make very decorative plants; fruit to eat in salads, or for cooking.

Best in: June–August, as the fruit grow.

Container: any. Size depends on number of plants.

Position: full sun or part shade.

Care: sow seed under warmth (glass) in late March, plant out after the frosts in May.

SPECIMEN ARCHITECTURAL PLANTS

Another effective idea for a container is to plant a single, spectacular plant in one and place it somewhere that will show it off to the best effect − against a contrasting wall, for example, or a dark hedge. I have chosen some plants that have either fascinating foliage, a dramatic shape or amazing blooms that make good specimen plants.

WRAP = If left outside for the winter, pots should be wrapped in hessian or bubble wrap to protect the roots from penetrating cold.

Melianthus major. Very decorative silver-green leaves but needs to be brought into the greenhouse or conservatory for the winter when it should be kept on the dry side.

Yucca gloriosa WRAP. Sculptural, stiff, sword-like leaves whose tips are needle sharp. These tips should be cut off to avoid injury, especially if there are children about. There is also a variegated form.

Cordyline australis (Cabbage palm). WRAP. A palm-like plant with graceful, floppy sword-like leaves. There is also a purple form.

Agapanthus 'Blue Giant' WRAP. One of many named varieties, with rounded heads of rich-blue tubular flowers in late summer and autumn. Agapanthus look very handsome in Versailles tubs, mainly because of their lush, arching, strap-shaped foliage.

Brassica oleracea (Ornamental cabbage). Cabbages infused with white, pink or red splashes. These annuals are most effectively grown in a

❀ MAY

large container surrounding a topiary box spiral or cone.

Phormium tenax 'Dazzler' (New Zealand Flax) WRAP. Arching bronze
   leaves striped in red, orange and pink.

Lilium regale. One of many lilies that do well in pots, ideal for
   bringing into the house when in full flower. The powerful scent
   spreads from room to room.

Plants for the forgetful waterer

The trouble with pots is that they dry out much more quickly than the
soil in the garden. Water evaporates faster from terracotta pots than
from plastic ones, but all plants in pots need consistent watering in
hot weather. This can be a problem for people who travel for work, go
away frequently at weekends or for anyone when they go on holiday,
not to mention people who are so busy they simply forget. All the
following aromatic plants will survive in a container for extended
periods without being watered.

Rosemary 'Benenden Blue'. A culinary rosemary with extra rich
   blue flowers.

Thymus x *citriodorus* '*Aureus*'. A lemon-scented thyme with
   gold-splashed leaves. One of the most ornamental of all the
   thymes.

Salvia officinalis 'Tricolor'. A sage with leaves splashed with cream,
   pink and purple.

Lavandula angustifolia 'Loddon Pink' (Lavender). A compact plant
   with soft pink flowers.

CONTAINER PLANTS FOR THE SHADE (AND SEMI-SHADE)

Sun-loving plants are grown so successfully in pots because they can
be placed in the sunniest, most sheltered spot, next to a wall perhaps
or where the sun beats on a terrace or balcony, and thrive on the heat.
If your garden or balcony does not face in a sunny direction, though,
there are still plants that you can grow successfully in containers and

which are very rewarding. Here are a few:

Hostas are one of the most rewarding perennials of all when grown in
   shaded positions. Choose species and varieties with large leaves
   like *H. sieboldiana* (glaucous blue), *H.* 'Sum and Substance' (yeLlow)
   or *H. undulata* var. *undulata* (twisted green leaves). Albomarginata
   (green with cream or pale yellow edges), whose leaves grow all
   the larger for being in the shade. Because hostas are so prone to
   snail and slug attack, leaving behind them ragged leaves, their pots
   should be raised on small stones or terracotta feet.
Acer shirasawanum 'Aureum' (used to be named *A. japonicum*
   'Aureum'). One of the most beautiful of all the ornamental maples.
   Small trees, with fan-shaped, bright yellow leaves.
Impatiens (Busy Lizzie). Of all the annuals, busy lizzies fare best in
   the shade without having to be watered every day.
Buxus sempervirens. Box is a remarkably tough and versatile
   evergreen shrub, tolerating even deep shade, where it can be
   clipped into a variety of shapes (see Topiary, page 112).

WINTER POTS

Pots can be made to work all year round, which is particularly worthwhile for the gardener whose whole garden is in containers. Here's an
idea for a container that would have something good to look at from
October to May.

Plant recipe: a central box topiary shape surrounded by the winter-
flowering ('Universal') pansy interplanted with crocuses (any colour),
tulips (Tulipa 'Apricot Beauty' — one of the most beautiful of all the
tulips) and daffodils (Narcissus 'Tête-à-Tête'— a dwarf, perfectly scaled
down version of the full large trumpet varieties), with ivy trailing
over the edge.
Effects: permanent topiary shape and ivy; tulips and daffodils in
early spring; pansies in spring and early summer.
Container: a large container, such as a wooden half-barrel.

MAY

Position: any sheltered, light spot. The more sun it gets, the earlier the bulbs will appear.

Care: regular watering during the warm months.

MINI PONDS

I am a firm believer that water can be introduced into even the smallest space, using a container. See the ideas on page 138.

PLANTERS FOR WALLS

The most amusing of these are those made of PVC, depicting a human face. I like to see them planted with a small, ornamental grass like Festuca glauca 'Blaufuchs' syn. 'Blue Fox' (bright blue leaves) or Carex elata 'Aurea' (Bowles' golden sedge — yellow leaves) to give them an amusing hair-do. This adds a touch of humour to the garden, always a welcome commodity.

HANGING BASKETS

Before planting a hanging basket, think ahead about the watering. There are devices to make watering hanging baskets easier, such as special pumping watering cans with long nozzles, pulleys to lower the baskets, water-absorbant crystals added to the bottom of the compost at root level, either dry or pre-soaked.

Today there is an ever-increasing number of plants with a cascading habit specially bred for hanging baskets and window boxes. Here are some ideas for planting:

Plant recipe 1: Glechoma hederacea 'Variegata' (trailing variegated ground ivy) — blue flowers and pretty foliage; Verbena 'Cascade White'; Bacopa 'Snowflake' (white); Felicia 'Read's Blue'; Helichrysum petiolare (silver leaves).

Effect: blue, white and silver.

Best in: June-August.

Position: sun or semi-shade.

Care: water and feed regularly.

MAY

Plant recipe 2: Ajuga reptans 'Burgundy Glow' (silver-green wine-red leaves). Although normally used as a ground cover plant, bugle will cascade from a basket; trailing snapdragon, Antirrhinum hispanicum 'Avelanche' (white); Diascia 'Ruby Fields' (shell-pink flowers); Nemesia 'Innocence' (white); Helichrysum petiolare (silver leaves).

Effect: pink, red, white and silver.

Best in: July–August.

Position: sun or semi-shade.

Care: water and feed regularly.

TIPS: CONTAINERS

❀ Ants sometimes nest in containers entering through the drainage hole and damaging root systems in the process. If containers are raised, using small stones or 'terracotta pot feet' (available at garden centres), the ants are denied easy access. Ants' nests, often found under large stones, are easily destroyed with boiling water.

❀ Empty or colourless gaps in borders can be filled temporarily by filling them with colourful or sculptural plants in containers.

❀ Give new terracotta pots an attractive, white bloom to make them look old and 'limed' by painting with very diluted white, water-based paint.

❀ Mend broken terracotta flower pots with Epoxy Resin. This is especially worthwhile if it is a big pot which is expensive to replace.

MAY

UNDERGROUND IRRIGATION

Although expensive to install, I think it is worth mentioning this method of watering as it does, in fact, make sense in the dryer summers we have had recently and is also pleasingly conservationist.

My hedging has proved expensive and, in order not to lose any of it to drought, I will be installing a 'leaky-hose' underground watering system for it. It is a fairly complex affair, involving joining a series of computerized taps to the mains water via yet another trench. The system then 'sweats' water from a porous pipe underground, ensuring that whatever is planted above it is kept well watered.

The licence for this system costs exactly the same as for a sprinkler, yet it uses far less water and uses it more efficiently as it leaks the water underground. Sprinklers are renowned for wasting a lot of water through evaporation on sunny days.

LAWNS

May is a good time to feed and care for your lawn. This is a vast subject, requiring a book of its own, but I will mention the most important facts and commonest problems here.

The attraction of a lawn is that it looks like a lovely green carpet, perfect for walking on in bare feet. Apart from giving children somewhere to play, lawns are also very practical as they need far less maintenance than borders. If you have limited time, the answer for a large garden is to seed or turf over such high-maintenance areas.

The perfect lawn

You have all seen the immaculate lawn that looks like green velvet and is mown into dark and pale perfect stripes. Creating a lawn like that is a specialist art and not one that many people aspire to. If you do, you have to devote a lot of time and energy to it and I suggest you read *The Lawn Expert* by Dr D. G. Hessayon, published by Transworld Publishers. I have never worried too much about my lawns being perfect in every way. In fact, I welcome the occasional daisy and turn a blind eye to a little moss. However, even I draw the line at dandelions, which seem to sense danger and grow as flat as they can, even producing stunted flowers in the hope that they can evade the blade. The leaves of plantains also lie flat and such weeds can always be removed by hand. I have too large an expanse of lawn to be able to do this and so I use a selective weedkiller which feeds the grasses and kills broad-leaved plants, using one application every other year or so.

 LAWN TIP

If you do aspire to good stripes on your lawn, always set your mower blades on the highest setting throughout summer. Grass left longer will show the marks of mowing in alternate directions more clearly. Even if you do not much care about stripes, longer grass always looks greener – in summer anyway.

Feeding

Feeding a lawn with a high-nitrogen feed any time from the end of April until the end of July gives it a boost but is not really necessary unless the lawn is looking very sorry for itself.

Aerating

Aerating an entire lawn or parts of it, either by hand with a fork or mechanically, in spring and autumn, is only a necessary chore if it becomes badly compacted due to constant use. You can hire mechanical aerators at hire shops.

Edges

Neat edges, cut with a half moon every spring, make all the difference to the look of a lawn. My grandmother always said that the most important part of a lawn was its neat edges. (She also always said, when asked how someone was, that they were either very well or dead!)

❁ MAY

Moss

As I have said, I would tolerate a small amount of moss. It is soft and usually bright green and not unattractive as long as it is not in large patches. You can treat moss with commercial products to kill it, but they leave behind a mass of unsightly dead growth for some time afterwards. If you have a lot of moss, it means the ground is badly drained. If water sits on the ground for some time after rainfall in summer and it is permanently soggy in winter it means it is very badly drained and will need remedial action – this will mean professional help with digging drains. Once the water is taken away to lower ground your problems should be solved. Isolated pockets of poorly drained ground can be remedied with a soak-away, a deep hole half-filled with large stones.

Rogue grasses

These are grass species that are often a lighter green than lawn grasses, tend to grow into hummocks and produce tall, spikey seed heads. The best way to deal with these is to slash them in a criss-cross with a sharp knife.

Hard-wearing lawns

In smaller gardens where there is not much room for a lawn, the turf can get very scuffed by the end of the summer. You may consider re-turfing or re-seeding your lawn with a grass mix capabale of better withstanding constant, heavy usage. These are available at comprehensive garden centres. It is a chore well worth the time and investment in the long run.

COPING WITH DROUGHT

With the threat of changing weather patterns hanging over us and the forecast that summers will become hotter and drier, it is just as well to

MAY ❁

plan accordingly, water conservation being a priority. Water is one of the most precious resources on our planet and every gardener should make efforts to collect it. Here are a few precautions you can take to combat the effects of drought conditions:

❀ Install water butts or tanks fed by down pipes from gutters for use in dry periods.

❀ Avoid using a hose or sprinkler when the sun is high in the sky as a high percentage of the water is lost through evaporation.

❀ Because newly planted trees and shrubs are at their most vulnerable during their first two seasons, it is best to plant them in a shallow basin so that when you water there is no surface run-off and all the water goes straight to the roots. This is good practice at any time, drought or no drought.

❀ Always dig bulky organic matter, well-rotted manure or garden waste into the soil around plants' roots. A soil with a good structure will retain moisture far better.

❀ Mulching (covering the soil surface around the base of plants when the soil is still wet) will conserve moisture in the soil as it helps to eliminate evaporation. All sorts of things can be used as a mulch – chipped bark, well-rotted organic matter, or even old carpet. Lawn clippings can also be used but only on established trees and shrubs.

❀ Water-retaining granules are particularly useful when it comes to plants in containers, especially hanging baskets or window boxes, although they can be used scattered among the roots on plants in the open. These are dry granules which can absorb hundreds of times their own volume of water. They can be applied dry or pre-wetted.

❀ Bath water, allowed to cool first, can be used on the garden and you can buy special devices that are attached to down pipes that divert the water. Water from dishwashers and washing machines contain harmful detergents and salts and should not be used.

❀ Get your priorities right. During dry spells water plants that need it most, like vegetable and fruit crops coming into season. Lawns, although they may turn brown, are not a priority, as they soon green

❀ MAY

up again when the late summer/autumn rains arrive.

❀ An automatic watering system can prove a godsend. When it comes to water conservation, the 'drip-irrigation' and 'leaky-hose' systems are efficient as little, if any, water is lost through evaporation. It is the water sprinklers left on in hot weather that rank amongst the worst of the water wasters.

❀ In areas of the garden which tend to become parched in summer you should think about growing plants whose leaves are adapted to such conditions. Most plants with grey or woolly leaves such as lamb's ear (*stachys*), lavender, senecio and rosemary are a few. The prime example of a plant that hates hot and dry conditions is the busy lizzie as all of its parts are sappy and fleshy.

Xerophytic plants

These are plants that thrive in dry spells in full sun and come from hot and dry parts of the world like California, South Africa and the Mediterranean. Some have thick waxy leaves, or silver leaves covered in fine hairs that are designed to cope with hot conditions. Here is a selection:

A = Annual HP = Herbaceous Perennial WS = Wall Shrub
SE = Semi Evergreen E = Evergreen

Armeria maritima (Thrift). A familiar small plant commonly seen
   growing in cracks on cliffs, with pink flowers in late spring and
   summer.
Centranthus ruber (Valerian). A self-seeding perennial with white,
   pink or red flowers in spring and summer.
Cistus (Rock rose). Many different shrubby species with white to dark
   pink flowers from mid to late summer. Rock roses are well suited to
   poor, dry, stony ground.
Dorotheanthus (Livingstone daisy). A wonderfully bright and
   colourful annual with white, crimson, red, gold or yellow flowers.

Eschscholzia californica (Californian poppy). A self-seeding annual
with flowers in shades of red, yellow and orange as well as white.

Fremontodendron californicum (Flannel bush). WS SE. Saucer shaped,
waxy flowers from late spring to autumn. In mild areas this can
be grown as a standard tree.

Helianthemum (Sun rose). A ground-hugging shrub with silver leaves
and white, red, salmon or pink flowers from late spring until
mid-summer.

Iris germanica (Bearded iris). Violet-blue flowers with yellow beards
in early summer and fans of grey-green leaves that remain
decorative throughout the rest of the summer.

Kniphofia (Red hot poker). Many different species with 'pokers' of red,
orange, yellow to green. 'Little Maid' is a smaller variety, with
pale yellow flowers in late summer and early autumn.

Lavandula (lavender). There are many different species and varieties
of this popular plant with flowers of purple, white or pink flower
L. angustifolia 'Hidcote' makes an excellent neat, low hedge.

Rosmarinus officinalis (Rosemary). Aromatic shrub with many
varieites including 'Tuscan Blue' (dark blue flowers) and 'Benenden
Blue' (vivid blue flowers).

Salvia officinalis (Common sage). An aromatic shrub with lilac-blue
flowers. *S. o.* 'Aurea', with yellowleaves is more compact.
There is also a purple and a variegated form.

Sedum spectabile (Ice plant) Irresistible to butterflies and bees, this
fleshy-leaved perennial has pink flowers in late summer.

MAY TASKS

❊ It should be safe to plant out tender annuals in the south after the
middle of this month, although you will have to wait until early June
in the north. If there is a threat of frost, protect plants with horticultural fleece.

❊ Moss on lawns can be raked out using a springbok rake.

❊ Start cutting asparagus on established plants and continue until

MAY

mid-summer's day (24 June). Some spears must be allowed to grow to allow the plant to photosynthesize, to build up its energies for the following season.

❀ Never venture out into the garden without green string and a sharp knife in your pocket. Plants are growing fast and there are always wayward shoots to tie in.

❀ A regular check on roses by looking at flower buds and the undersides of leaves may well reveal the first appearance of greenfly. If you catch them early you will avoid serious infestations later on. Spraying to prevent rather than cure is always a good idea, although they can be rubbed off by hand.

❀ Towards the end of the month, formal box hedges can be given a light clip.

❀ Sweetcorn can be planted out at the end of the month. They are best planted in blocks rather than in rows to ensure better cross-pollination.

❀ Pinch out side shoots on tomatoes as they appear, unless they are bush varieties.

❀ Dead-head daffodils by pulling the seed heads off and allow the plants to die back naturally.

❀ Lift tulip bulbs and store them in a cool, dry place for replanting in November.

❀ Sow brussels sprouts for the Christmas feast.

MAY ❀

Here comes summer

JUNE

IF THIS IS GLOBAL WARMING then I do not suppose we have much to worry about. It is more like global freezing. Everything is about a month late. The last of the daffodils faded in mid-May and the ash trees look as bare as they did in January, from a distance.

It has been hellish gardening weather. During a rare dry spell I sprayed the large garden for the second time with Roundup to get rid of a mass of remaining nettles and couch grass. I did this three weeks prior to the return of the excavating machine to give them enough time in which to wither. June heralded warmer, drier weather and Tim, the JCB operator, returned. We only managed to complete the levelling around the round pond and the trenching for the round hedge, but I am well pleased as now, for the first time, the shape of the large garden is starting to emerge.

We trenched two feet deep and just over one foot wide. This will allow for good and deep soil preparation and will give me plenty of room in which to install a 'leaky pipe' automatic irrigation system below ground. Tim put the clay and stone into separate heaps from the good top soil so that they can be removed by lorry when he next returns later this month to continue with the trenching. This area is known for its shallow clay, so it came as a relief that my top soil averages two feet, with only a few inches of clay at the bottom of one section of the trenches. Once the hedges are planted they will be mulched with shredded bark, something I use in borders and around individual shrubs and trees as well. It lasts longer than most other mulches because of its woody consistency, it blends in beautifully and is an excellent weed supressor.

The cross axis path running north/south across the lawned path leading towards the pond from the house has taken some considerable thought. I eventually opted for pavers in various hues of over-fired terracotta. These are delightfully small, measuring 160 x 80 x 40mm, which I intend laying in herringbone. Smaller pavers always create richer patterns.

JUNE ❀

Encourage daisies, forget-me-nots, buttercups and other wild flowers.

June 12. Yes, summer has arrived and with it cow parsley and hawthorn along the road verges and fields full of flowering clovers, ox-eye daisies and buttercups. It is such a pity that local councils decide to cut back cow parsley in country lanes when it is in full splendour. I have strimmed around the base of the trees and shrubs at the front of the house as most of them are still babies, but I have encouraged the daisies, nodding grasses, forget-me-nots, dead nettles and buttercups to enjoy their freedom. The cuckoo is singing on a still, warm evening. I wish it weren't quite so noisy at 4am.

I have been moving spring bulbs for summer storage in the cool of the barn, for replanting this autumn. They needed moving because they were in the wrong place and included red and yellow tulips, single early types that seem to naturalize, and 'Tête-à-Tête', my favourite of all the daffodils. I had taken the precaution of photographing them when in flower so I knew exactly where they all were. Accordingly, I have put them in separate, labelled large black plastic flower pots half full of top soil. I have also dug up blind daffodil clumps whose soil had obviously become deprived of goodness and these I shall replant with extra TLC, with leaf mould worked into the soil and a sprinkling of Osmocote to ensure they flower next year.

I have been busy tying back climbers, very much a June job. My autumn-planted *Rosa* 'Compassion', one of the best scented of all the climbing roses, with salmon-pink flowers tinted with apricot-orange, has grown apace. I have also been wiring walls for climbers, using screw eyes and galvanized wire. Climbers are then easily tied onto the wires with raffia or soft string. Tucking climbers in *behind* wires, as people often do, means that the wires have to be cut when the climber dies, as opposed to snip, snip, snip with the secateurs and the whole thing falls neatly away leaving the wire intact.

Chelsea Flower Show was the blowiest and wettest ever this year. Indeed at one stage the huge marquee had to be evacuated owing to ominous creaks in the rafters. Going to Chelsea Flower Show is like going to see a good film. The first time it is exciting but it becomes increasingly less gripping on successive visits. However, it is fun watching and overhearing the people and their opinions and this is a snippet I picked up this year: there were two rather distinguished ladies visiting Chelsea Flower Show for the first time. As they were being pushed along in the jostling crowds one turned to the other and said, 'Of course if it wasn't so crowded many more people would come.' I find it a sobering thought that gardens at Chelsea, which can

JUNE

cost more than £100,000 to stage, are on view for a mere five days.

I never let anything go to waste. I have found an excellent use for some scaffolding planks, left behind from the work on the house. I have used five 6ft planks, braced together sitting on sturdy wooden 'A' frame trestle feet, to make an excellent outdoor table which can be left out in all weathers and looks a million dollars. It is perfect under the damson in the far corner of the back garden where there is welcome shade on a hot summer's day. We cannot imagine how we lived without it before. The ferns planted around the table at the base of the high wall make perfect soulmates for the young ivy growth popping through the wall and I have interspersed them with stone *objets d'art*. My favourite of all the ferns remains the Shuttlecock fern (*Matteuccia struthiopteris*) because of the way its fronds are so neatly arranged and the fact that it stands to attention more than most ferns. I am slowly collecting more and have recently planted two more unusual types, *Dryopteris affinis* 'Cristata the King' and *Athyrium felix-femina* 'Frizelliae'.

All the seeds Rosie, my youngest daughter, sowed in March have popped up a treat – tomatoes, annual asters, schizanthus and salpiglossis. I have planted them out for her in her own place close to the new terrace. I used to do the same thing when I was the same age but had to be sent photographs of them in flower because the summer term at boarding school seemed to last for ever and we were not allowed home during term time. Barbaric! Rosie is going to sell some of her plants at a car boot sale this Sunday. A sense of commerce – good for her.

TAKING PHOTOGRAPHS

When you live with a garden you never realize quite how much it changes from year to year and how fast plants grow. It is the same with children. It is people who see them only from time to time who can see how they change and grow. Not only will photographs prove fascinating in later years, but they will also tell you how fast plants grow and remind you of how various different parts of the garden can be improved at different times of the year.

JUNE WEEDING

Along with all the glorious flowers that June brings comes the weeds which grow at an alarming speed. Weeding is no one's favourite chore and there are ways of reducing their number. The three best ways of reducing the weed population are:

❀ Planting ground cover plants: (see page 24).
❀ Regular hoeing: this uproots some small weeds and beheads others, effectively killing them. It is not a back-breaking job and is very satisfying, leaving the soil bare and tidy. It is a pleasurable job for a dry day.
❀ Mulching: cover the ground with a 10cm (4in) layer of organic matter to smother germinating weeds.

TIP: A WAY TO CLEAR NEGLECTED GROUND
In early spring, smother the surface with a 15cm (6in) layer of well-rotted organic matter and over this lay a plastic sheet secured with weights. By the following spring you can start planting, although leaving it until autumn will ensure that even the most pernicious perennial weeds will have been killed by suffocation. The mulch will improve soil structure at the same time.

❀ JUNE

CLIMBING PLANTS

Climbing plants are the wallpaper of the garden. Whereas attention is always paid to the clothing of horizontal surfaces in a garden, many of the vertical surfaces are forgotten or at least not always given sufficient attention. Climbing plants can give interest and colour at a height, cover an ugly fence and generally soften the outlines of a garden, particularly a rectangular town garden. They can be trained through shrubs and trees and chosen to flower when the shrub or tree is not performing so that part of the garden still has interest.

Climbers come in all shapes, colours and sizes. They climb by several different methods. Some twine around anything slender and twiggy (Clematis, for example), some self-cling with modified roots or adhesive pads (this includes Ivy) and others need to be tied to supports (roses). You need to know how they climb so you can provide the appropriate support.

Most climbers are perennial, although there are a few annuals. There is a bewilderingly large choice, so I have whittled them down to my favourites only, those that I have grown and liked.

Here is a selection of climbers for a sunny aspect:

H = approximate Height E = Evergreen T = Twining climber
SC = Self-clinging

Actinidia kolomikta H4m (13ft) T. Leaves generously splashed in white
  and pink. I have seen one growing happily over a north-facing,
  therefore shaded, porch where the variegation was predominantly
  pink.
Actinidia deliciosa 'Jenny' (Chinese gooseberry; Kiwi fruit)
  H60 m (20ft) T. Ornamental leaves and red, hairy young shoots,
  bearing fruits in late summer. This is a hermaphrodite
  variety, meaning that you do not have to plant a male and
  a female plant in order to get fruit.
Campsis x tagliabuana 'Mme Galen', H6m (20ft) SC. Orange-pink
  trumpets from summer to autumn.
Clematis armandii H6m (20ft) E, T. Scented white flowers in early
  spring and attractive evergreen foliage.
Hedera helix 'Buttercup' (Golden-leaved ivy) H6m (20ft) SC E.

JUNE

Rich butter-yellow leaves. In many ways the most decorative of all the ivies. Very effective when grown up the trunk of an established deciduous tree and kept cut at about 1m (3ft).

Jasminum officinale 'Fiona Sunrise' H not known as it has not been in cultivation for long T. A variety of common jasmine with striking yellow leaves. Tolerant of semi-shade.

Lonicera japonica 'Halliana' (Honeysuckle) H10m (30ft) E, T. Strongly scented white flowers ageing to pale yellow.

Parthenocissus tricuspidata (Boston ivy) H20m (65ft) SC. Spectacular crimson autumn colour. Very useful for covering large walls.

Passiflora caerulea (Passion flower) H5m (16ft) T. White purple and blue flowers in mid-summer until autumn. After a hard winter all top growth can be killed off but it normally starts to produce shoots again from the base, sometimes as late as July. This plant was named by early Spanish missionaries in South America who likened the flowers to the Passion of Christ. The ten sepals represent the apostles excluding Peter and Judas; the purple corona the crown of thorns; the five anthers the five wounds; the three stigmas the three nails and the tendrils the whips that chastised Him.

Schizophragma integrifolium H12m (40ft) SC. White flat flowers with spearhead-shaped outer sterile florets in late summer and autumn.

Trachelospermum jasminoides (Star jasmine) H6m (20ft) E. Not showy, but the small white flowers are hard to beat for strength of scent.

Vitis vinifera 'Purpurea' (Vine) H4.5m (15ft) T. A superb ornamental vine with reddish, rich purple leaves. *V coignetiae* (Crimson glory vine).

Wisteria sinensis 'Alba' H7.5m (25ft) T. Scented, pure white flowers in spring.

Perennial climbers

Perennial climbers prefer sunny aspects and die back completely in the winter. They can be used to great effect when encouraged to

JUNE

scramble in amongst established trees and shrubs and look especially effective clothing conifers. Some of my favourites are:

Humulus lupulus 'Aureus' (Golden hop) H6m (20ft) T. Rich display of pale yellow-green leaves.

Lathyrus grandiflorus (Everlasting pea) H1.5m (5ft) T. Pink-purple, red or white flowers in summer.

Tropaeolum speciosum (Flame creeper; Flame nasturtium) H3m (10ft) T. Scarlet flowers in summer.

Annual climbers for sunny aspects

These can be encouraged to scramble through established shrubs or hedges:

Cobaea scandens (Cup-and-saucer vine) H4m (11ft) T. Unusual yellow-green flowers ageing to purple. *C.s. alba* is the white form.

Ipomoea hederacea (Morning glory) H3m (10ft) T. Funnel-shaped purple or blue flowers in summer and early autumn.

Tropaeolum tuberosum 'Ken Aslet', H2m (6ft) T. Red and orange flowers from mid-summer to autumn. Lift and store tubers in winter.

Eccremocarpus scaber (Chilean glory flower) H2m (6ft) T. Orange-red flowers followed by decorative fruit pods.

Lathyrus odoratus (Sweet pea) 2m (6ft) T. Sweetly scented flowers in summer and early autumn. There are countless named varieties to choose from, covering the entire colour spectrum except black. Very useful for growing up cane tripods towards the back of the border. If they are allowed to form seed heads and are not dead-headed on a regular basis they will cease flowering.

Climbing roses

The climbing roses represent some of the most rewarding of all climbing plants. In order to keep them neat and tidy, new shoots should be tied in regularly during summer, normally onto horizontal wires. The following are listed by the Royal National Rose Society who consider them to be 'Roses of Special Merit' (1997). They have been chosen for their general all-round garden value. Most are reasonably disease-resistant, repeat flower and are easy to look after. They are all suitable for sunny walls, fences, arches, pillars and pergolas. (There is more information about other kinds of roses on pages 188-196.) Here is a selection:

H = Height S = Spread

'Aloha' H3m (10ft) S1.8m (6ft). Strongly fragrant, sumptuous, rose-pink and magenta flowers all summer.

'Bantry Bay' H3.5m (12ft) S2.5m (8ft). Scented, semi-double, deep pink flowers most of the summer. Very free-flowering.

'Calypso' (also known as 'Blush Boursault') H4.5m (15ft) S3m (10ft). Slightly fragrant, fully double, blush pink flowers.

'Climbing Arthur Bell' H3.5m (12ft) S2.5m (8ft). Very fragrant deep yellow, double flowers paling to soft yellow.

'Compassion' H3m (10ft) S1.8m (6ft). Very fragrant, apricot and copper flowers with yellow highlights.

'Dortmund' H2.5m (8ft) S1.8m (6ft). A profusion of single, red flowers with a white centre. Suitable for a north-facing wall.

'Dublin Bay' H2m (7ft) S1.5m (5ft). Clusters of slightly fragrant, rich blood-red flowers all summer.

'Golden Showers' H3m (10ft) S1.8m (6ft). Slightly fragrant deep golden-yellow flowers fading to cream from June to October.

'Highfield' H 2.5m (8ft) S1.8m (6ft). Very fragrant flowers similar to 'Compassion' but less brash.

'Leaping Salmon' H3m (10ft) S1.8m (6ft). Fragrant, large salmon-pink flowers.

'New Dawn' H3m (10ft) S2.5m (8ft). Strongly scented, semi-double, blush-pink flowers from June to October. An outstanding rose.

❀ JUNE

'Pink Perpétué' H3.5m (12ft) S2.5m (8ft). Moderately fragrant,
   semi-double, pink flowers throughout summer. One of the best.
'Rosy Mantle' 2.5 x 2.5m (8 x 8ft). Strongly scented, silver-pink, fully
   double flowers.
'Summer Wine' H3m (10ft) S1.8m (6ft). Moderately fragrant, large,
   semi-double, deep pink flowers.
'Sympathie' H3m (10ft) S2.5m (8ft). Fragrant, fully double, dark red
   flowers throughout summer.

TIP

 If red-flowering roses are grown up against red brick walls
some of the colour impact is lost. White or yellow-flowering
varieties would be a better choice. For the same reason red,
pink and yellow roses stand out all the better against a
white surface.

FIND THAT ROSE

Have you ever tried to identify a rose? It is not always easy. There are
literally thousands. I inherited five climbers of the same species planted up against a boundary wall in front of the house, with masses of
single red, but sadly unscented, flowers. Which rose is it? 'Dortmund'.
I found the easiest and quickest source of reference to be *The Rose
Expert* by Dr D.G. Hessayon. This is the name of a catalogue listing
almost 3,000 roses, to help you locate roses from over 70 growers.
Write to: The Editor, *Find That Rose*, 303 Mile End Road, Colchester,
Essex CO4 5EA.

Rose, rose and clematis
Trail and twine and clasp and kiss
          'The clematis and the rose' (Tennyson)

One disadvantage of most climbing roses is that they tend to become
bare and leggy at the base, with most of the leaf and flower at the

JUNE

top. An effective way of overcoming this problem is to plant a clematis that flowers at the same time as the rose at its base. The mid-blue flowers of clematis 'Mrs Cholmondeley' complement the shell pink flowers of the rose 'New Dawn' and the deep violet flowers of the clematis 'Etoile Violette' mix well with the pink flowers of the rose 'Pink Perpétué'. Clematis is also very useful in giving spring — and early-summer-flowering shrubs like lilac and philadelphus — a second lease of life.

Cutting back clematis

Confusion reigns about when to cut back different species of clematis as there exist so many different species and varieties under a bewildering list of different groups. There is one simple rule to follow: 'If it flowers before June, do not prune.'

Cool clematis

Clematis must have their roots in the shade and be kept cool if they are to do well. They love the sort of shaded conditions found at the base of a low north-facing wall, or else plant a shrub on their south side, or place flagstones or gravel over the soil surrounding the roots.

Here are some climbers for a north-facing or shaded wall:

H = Height E = Evergreen T = Twining climber S = Self-clinging

Clematis alpina H3m (10ft) T. Lantern-shaped, blue flowers in spring, fluffy, silvery seed heads in summer. Good exposed sites.

Hedera helix 'Glacier' (Ivy) H3m (10ft) E SC. Silver-marbled leaves. Useful for a dark corner.

Hydrangea anomala ssp. petiolaris (Climbing hydrangea) H15m (50ft) SC. Heads of lacy white flowers in summer. Very useful for a north-facing wall or clothing the bare trunk of a mature, deciduous tree.

❧ JUNE

Jasminum nudiflorum (Winter jasmine) H3m (10ft). Yellow flowers on
   bare stems throughout winter. Needs to be tied onto a support.
Jasminum officinale (Common white jasmine) H12m (40ft) T. Scented
   white flowers in summer and autumn.
Lonicera x americana (Honeysuckle) H6m (20ft) T. Strongly scented
   yellow flowers, flushed with red-purple.
Rosa 'Madame Alfred Carriere' H4.5m (15ft). Strongly scented
   large, white, sometimes pink-tinged flowers. Needs to be tied onto
   a support.
Rosa 'Danse du Feu' H3.5m (12ft). Bright brick-red flowers most of
   the summer. Needs to be tied onto a support.

There are two climbing plants that should never be entertained in a
small to medium-sized garden because they are too vigorous and
eventually take up too much space:

Russian or Mile-a-Minute vine (*Fallopia baldschaunica* – used to
   be named *Polygonum baldschaunicum*), a deciduous twining
   plant with white flowers in late summer which, once established,
   is capable of growing 20 feet or more a year, smothering shrubs
   and small trees as it gallops along not only in your garden
   but also in your neighbours'. It should only be planted under
   exceptional circumstances, to cover something large like an
   ugly out-building.
Kiftsgate rose (*Rosa filipes* 'Kiftsgate'), the most vigorous of all
   the climbing roses with huge, cascading trusses of scented,
   creamy-white flowers in mid-summer. This beautiful rose grows
   much too large for most walls. It can, however, be encouraged
   to grow up and through a very large tree. This has been done
   in the garden where it was bred at Kiftsgate Court in
   Gloucestershire, where it has become the largest rose in England,
   climbing up a copper beech to an estimated height of
   15m (50ft).

COPING WITH CLAY

I am very lucky, given that I am in an area notorious for clay, in that my topsoil is deep and crumbly, with no sign of clay at all. But if you have heavy, clay soil, do not despair. There are many plants that will do well on clay and you can work to improve the soil over the years. If you find you have solid clay with little if any top soil, the best thing to do is to remove it all down to about two feet and bring in fresh top soil. This can prove to be an enormous undertaking and is really only to be used as a desperate measure.

The reason that clay is not a good medium in which to grow most plants is because it is made up of tiny particles that stick together so tightly that they do not allow any oxygen (essential for plant growth) into the soil.

There are several ways to get around your clay problem. Dig individual holes for trees and shrubs, refilling them with fresh top soil and well-rotted organic matter as you go. Do this even if your plant is tolerant of clay, to get it off to a better start. For herbaceous perennials and especially vegetables, it is often easier to build raised beds and borders filled with fresh top soil. Deeper ones can be built of stone or brick and shallower ones of about 30cm (12in) in depth of wooden planks secured with pegs.

To improve the soil, double-digging, incorporating well-rotted organic matter down to a depth of two spits of the spade is another alternative, although you will need a very strong back if you are digging over a large area.

Some people decry digging, as they argue that it destroys a soil's structure, and suggest regular mulching with organic matter as an alternative. This succeeds in slowly building up an easily workable top soil but it will take many years to achieve a sufficiently deep friable surface to work with. I have seen splendid long and strong root vegetables grown in ground treated this way, so I know it works.

❧ JUNE

Here is a selection of trees for clay soils:

H = approximate Height E = Evergreen S/E = Semi-Evergreen

Acer campestre (Native maple; Field maple) H15m (50ft). Rosy or
  pinky red leaves in spring.
Carpinus betulus (Common hornbeam) H25m (82ft). An excellent
  alternative to beech which it resembles in leaf. *C. b.* 'Fastigiata',
  the upright growing form, is a good choice for the smaller garden.
Eucalyptus gunnii (Cider gum) H25m (82ft) E. Blue-green leaves and
  decorative peeling bark. Fast-growing, but not suitable for a windy
  site as it tends to become top-heavy.
Laburnum x *wateri* 'Vossii' (Voss' laburnum) H15m (50ft). Hanging
  chains of yellow flowers in late spring and early summer.
Malus hupehensis (Hupeh crab apple) H7.5m (25ft). White, scented
  flowers in spring followed by yellow crab apples. All the crab
  apples and larger fruiting apples grow in clay soils.
Populus x *candicans* 'Aurora' (Poplar) H15m (50ft). Very fast growing
  with leaves blotched creamy-white.
Prunus 'Pandora' (Flowering cherry) H10m (30ft). Masses of pale pink
  flowers in early spring. Good autumn colour. All flowering cherries
  grow in clay soils.
Salix babylonica var. *pekinensis* 'Tortuosa' (Dragon's-claw willow)
  H12m (40ft). Twisted twigs and branches.
Sorbus aucuparia (Mountain ash; Rowan) H12m (40ft). White
  flowers in spring and red berries in autumn. Good autumn colour.

Here is a selection of shrubs for clay soils:

Abelia x *grandiflora* 3 x 3m (10 x 10ft) S/E. Masses of pink-tinged,
  white flowers from summer to autumn.
Berberis thunbergii (Barberry) H2m (6ft) S3m (10ft). Red-tinged, pale
  yellow flowers in spring. Good autumn colour, scarlet berries.
Buddleja davidii 'Harlequin' 3 x 3m (10 x 10ft). Red-purple flowers

from mid-summer to autumn and creamy-white variegated leaves.
Many other varieties to choose from.

Buxus (Common box) 5 x 5m (15 x 15ft) E. Invaluable for topiary or
screening.

Corylus maxima 'Purpurea' (Purple-leaved filbert) H6m (20ft) S5m
(15ft). Purple/yellow catkins in late winter and edible nuts in
autumn.

Hibiscus syriacus is prized for its flowers in late summer.

Forsythia x *intermedia* 'Lynwood 3 x 3m (10 x 10ft). An
abundance of yellow flowers in spring. A popularly grown variety.

Garrya ellitica 'James Roof' (Silk-tassel bush) 4 x 4m (12 x 12ft)
E. Grey-green, long tassels from mid-winter to early spring.

Hibiscus syriacus, H3m (10ft) S2m (6ft). There are a number of
varieties of this shrub prized for its flowers in late summer. 'Blue
Bird' has large lilac-blue flowers with red centres and 'Red Heart'
white flowers with showy red centres.

JUNE

Hydrangea quercifolia (Oak-leaved hydrangea) 1.5 x 1.5m (5 x 5ft). Decorative foliage and white flowers in late summer. Hydrangeas like damp soils and get their name from hydor, Greek for water.

Juniperus x *media* 'Pfitzeriana' (Juniper) H2m (6ft) S3m (10ft) E. One of the most successful weed-supressors. Needs plenty of space.

Lavandula angustifolia 'Hidcote' (Lavender) H60cm (2ft) S75cm (30in). Fragrant purple flowers in midsummer. This particular lavender has a neat shape and is a perfect choice for a low hedge.

Philadelphus 'Beauclerk' (Mock orange) 2.5 x 2.5m (8 x 8ft). Strongly scented white flowers in midsummer.

Phormium tenax (New Zealand flax) H2m (6ft) S1m (3ft). Rigid, upright leaves and 4m (12ft) tall dull red flowers on the top of tall stalks once the plant has matured. Surprisingly hardy considering its exotic looks.

Pyracantha rogersiana (Firethorn) 4 x 4m (12 x 12ft). Beautifully scented white flowers in summer and red berries much favoured by birds. Countless different species and varieties.

Syringa vulgaris (Common lilac) 6 x 6m (20 x 20ft). There are many different types of lilac but at the end of the day there's little to beat the delicious scent of the white flowers of the common lilac.

Viburnum plicatum 'Mariesii' H3m (10ft) S4m (13ft). Distinctly tiered horizontal branches covered in white flowers in summer. There exist a great many other viburnums, some winter-flowering and many with scented flowers, all of them being tolerant of clay soils.

Weigela 'Bristol Ruby' H3m (10ft) S2m (6ft). Masses of scarlet flowers in early summer. There are many others to choose from.

JUNE TASKS

❀ Once the fourth truss of flowers has been formed on tomatoes, the leading shoot is best removed so that the plant can ripen all the fruits.

❀ Water sweet peas in dry spells, keep them fed regularly and pick flowers as they come out.

❀ Treat hard-working roses to liquid feeds.

❀ Cut out weak shoots on raspberries at ground level to give breathing space for the strong new shoots.

❀ Apply a nitrogen-rich feed to pale, yellowing lawns.

❀ Keep the base of hedges clear of weeds to prevent bare gaps from forming through lack of light.

❀ Take cuttings of garden pinks, or 'pipings', from non-flowering shoots, in a sandy medium.

❀ Make your own pot-pourri using scented flowers of lavender, roses and pinks, mixed with leaves or aromatic plants like eau-de-cologne mint and lemon verbena.

❀ Give aubretias a haircut by cutting off dead flowers with shears.

❀ Start cutting and storing herbs for winter use. Herbs can be dried by hanging them in bunches upside down in an airy, cool shed or garage, or chopped finely and frozen in ice cubes for stews.

❀ Take cuttings of tender geraniums and fuchsias, as well as hydrangea this month.

❀ Foxgloves are more likely to perennate if flower spikes are cut out the minute the flowers have faded.

❀ Cut flower spikes on lupins back to any side flower shoots for a longer display

❀ 'Rogue' grasses in lawns can be slashed criss-cross with an old kitchen knife. Repeated attacks will eventually get rid of them.

❀ Dead-head flowers on rhododendrons without damaging the young shoots directly below. A sticky job for the patient gardener.

❀ Give houseplants a holiday in a shaded part of the greenhouse. Repot them if necessary and keep them well fed and watered.

❀ Continue to tie in new, pliable shoots on climbers.

❀ The best time to cut lavender for drying or pot pourri is just as the flowers are opening and their aromatic oil content is highest.

❀ Dig up spring flowering bulbs in containers to make way for bedding plants.

❀ Cut out flower spikes of iris after flowering. The leaves can be left since they are so ornamental, although they can be reduced by a third if they start to brown at the tips.

JUNE

Roses come in all shapes and sizes.

A profusion of flowers

JULY

MOST OF THE SUMMER HAS BEEN SPENT gardening with a JCB, pick-axe and sledgehammer. Between them they have wreaked havoc, a necessary mess in order to give my new plants the best possible start in life. The trenches for my hedging in the main garden are now complete. However, I have had to cut my coat according to my cloth, and have considerably reduced the amount of hedging in this garden since it was going to cost me so much in plants and labour. The ever-important round yew hedge with its wings (which form the backbone to the garden) and the curving beech hedge on the edge of the drive still remain. Despite the fact that I have been able to source hedging plants at cost, they are still going to cost me well over £1,000 and that doesn't include costs for the installation of the automatic watering system and labour.

I raised a tray of seedlings of *Erigeron karvinskianus* (syn *E. mucronatus*), sold as *Erigeron* 'Profusion' in my local garden centre and I have been planting them out. I was first inspired by this plant in Prince Peter Wolkonsky's garden, at Kerdalo in Brittany, where they grew in a great frothing foam of white and pink flowers tumbling down some stone steps. He used to propagate them very successfully by wrapping ripe seed in small balls of clay and then stuffing them into cracks in paving and wall in late summer.

Erigeron has something in common with *Iris unguicularis* which produces glorious rich purple flowers in autumn and spring, ideal for cutting. They both like poor, mortar-rich, dry soil, although this iris likes growing at the base of a hot, sunny wall. We can all be grateful that two such beautiful flowers should like such inhospitable conditions as most gardens have them somewhere. I have planted my erigeron under the drawing-room window, close up to the wall, where the soil, if you can call it that, is all the things it likes.

I have started to excavate the formal topiary farm animal garden ready for planting this autumn. The soil is extremely poor, consisting mostly of sand and pebbles. I have therefore had to dig trenches 30cm (1ft) deep and about as wide, in which I will put plenty of well-rotted horse manure to give the dwarf box (*Buxus sempervirens* 'Suffruticosa') hedging and the common box, yew and ivy, which will be clipped and trained into the shapes of animals, a good, rich start. I must order another skip, the eighteenth to date. The wall adjoining the topiary gardens is smothered with the rich, red flowers of *Rosa* 'Dortmund', which looks glorious.

The paved area outside the large windows at the back of the house is a perfect spot for plants in containers. It is difficult to grow anything in the ground, as the old cellar, now filled in, is below. Apparently, this was an ideal cellar for keeping beer in the wood, as a stream used to flow across the floor, keeping the beer a perfect temperature during the summer months. Over the years I have collected old terracotta pots of all sizes which I have grouped together and have filled with some favourite plants.

In the smallest pot is a tiny mint (*Mentha requenii*), with leaves about 1mm ($^1/_{32}$in) across and wide, which grow into a small carpet. In July it is peppered in tiny blue flowers of roughly the same size and makes for a perfect plant for a trough garden. The brightest colour is supplied by tender geraniums which I got in France. On holiday two years ago we were driving through a village called Saint Jory de Chalais near Perigueux when we passed a house festooned from top to toe with geraniums. I knocked on the front door and it was answered

by a sweet little old lady with white hair swept up into a bun and little round black-framed glasses, the sort you never see in England
these days.

I merely wanted to congratulate her on her wonderful display, but
before I knew what was happening she was tearing off bits of all of
them to give to me. I haven't had them named, but the flowers are so
much more vibrant somehow than those commonly sold. *Melianthus
major*, with its beautifully shaped silver foliage is there, a plant Beth
Chatto grows successfully in her frost pocket in Essex, despite the fact
that it hails from South Africa. I saw it in flower in Morocco this
April, with striking, strong red flowers on tall stems.

In other pots are mixed *diascias* in colours ranging from shell to
salmon pink, green-flowering *nicotiana* and, my favourite of all the
osteospermums 'Stardust', with white flowers with a metallic blue
centre and variegated leaves. In the very corner, growing in a pot on
a column, is a variegated *agave* which I have now had for six years,
next to a large wooden half-barrel full of apple mint and fraise de
bois. In one of my largest pots is an *agapanthus* that grows wild on
the island of Tresco. When I went there they were bulldozing them
out of the ground in vast quantities and then selling them for £2 each
by the exit gate!

My most special plant here is a self-seeding annual, *Nicandra
physaloides*, given to me by Andrew Haines, the head gardener at
Edmonsham House near Cranborne in Dorset. It has fascinating leaves
covered in tiny, pin-prick-sized black dots and blue, bell-shaped flowers with a white throat. It is a reliable self-seeder, even in the poorest
soil. The walled gardens at Edmonsham are run organically and very
beautiful they are too.

A TIMELY HAIRCUT

There are some plants which, as the summer wears on, can benefit
from a trim. Plants I do this to include:

JULY

Stachys byzantina (Lamb's ears). In a sunny border it spreads into a woolly, silver cushion. However, it then produces 60cm (2ft) tall, woolly, pink-purple flowers in June which soon start to fall over. I cut the flower stalks down low to a pair of small leaves in June before the flowers open. These stems can be used in the house and the plant soon bounces back and becomes a neat silver cushion once more.

Alchemilla mollis (Lady's mantle). One of the most rewarding plants of all for its decorative rounded pale green leaves in which water droplets sit like jewels, and yellow fluffy flower heads in mid-summer, it is best cut back with a pair of shears to within a few inches of ground level just as the flowers begin to fade. Lovely as it is, it will self-seed all over the place given half a chance. The flowers can be dried for the winter vase and the plant will regrow into a neat plant again in late summer.

Two other ground cover herbaceous perennials that also take on a second lease of life if cut right back after flowering are the cranesbills (Geranium species and varieties) and the horned violet (*Viola cornuta*). If you are lucky and the conditions are right, these may flower a second time, giving you extra value.

THE ROSE GARDEN

Gardens should be full of fulfilled dreams. My ideal rose garden would be a smallish area surrounded by a tall wall or hedge designed

JULY

> TIP: PLANTING ROSES
>
> Roses like plenty of well-rotted manure around their roots if they are to get off to a good start, as well as an annual mulch of the same thereafter. One little knack I picked up from Percy, my aunt's gardener in Sark, is to stab the sides of the hole you dig for your roses with a fork before you fill it with manure-enriched compost. This softens the sides, especially in heavy soils, to make root penetration easier.

to trap the scent, filled with scented roses interplanted with hostas, lavender and honeysuckle, their best companion plants.

Choosing roses

There are so many different roses available these days, with new kinds appearing every year as a result of a busy breeding programme world-wide, that it is difficult to make the right choice. Choosing roses from photographs in catalogues or books is one way of picking out a rose, although the colour reproduction is sometimes inaccurate. I find it far better to go to a nursery or leading flower show to see the actual flowers for real, where hundreds are all grown or shown together, making choice far easier by comparison and by the fact that you can smell the scent yourself. One of the best nurseries to visit is that of David Austin Roses Ltd, Bowling Green Lane, Albrighton, Wolverhampton, WV7 3HB, 10 miles west of Wolverhampton.

'English' roses

Apart from climbers (see pages 174-177), ramblers and bush roses there are ground cover roses, hedging roses and even miniature and patio roses. The most exciting and rewarding garden roses to have emerged in recent years are called 'English roses'. These are bushes bred by David Austin, who recognized the potential of crossing old-fashioned roses from the eighteenth and nineteenth centuries – the Gallicas, Damasks, Portland and Bourbon roses, with the more modern hybrid teas and floribundas. The resulting mixed blood has the charm and the scent of the former combined with the wider colour range and repeat flowering ability of the latter and is a range of outstanding roses with luscious, often strongly scented flowers in many colours that continue all summer long. Amongst the best of these are :

'Evelyn' ('Tamora' x 'Graham Thomas') H120cm (4ft) S90cm (3ft). Very large, very double (about 130 petals per flower), strongly

❁ JULY

scented, apricot flowers.

'L.D. Braithwaite' ('The Squire' x 'Mary Rose') 1 x 1m (3ft 6in x 3ft 6in). Large, double, scarlet flowers with old rose scent.

'Glamis Castle' ('Graham Thomas' x 'Mary Rose') H90cm (3ft) S75cm (3½ft). Deeply cupped, white flowers with a myrrh scent.

'Eglantyne Jebb' ('Mary Rose' x unnamed seedling) H1m (3ft 6in) S 90cm (3ft). Very double, scented, soft pink flowers. (You will see that the blood of 'Mary Rose', with double pink flowers and 'Graham Thomas' with rich deep-yellow flowers, are popular choices as parent plants. This is because they hand down to their offspring their strong genetic characteristics of vigour, the ability to produce abundant flowers throughout the summer and disease resistance.)

COMMERCIAL SUCCESS?

❀ It takes seven whole years until a newly bred rose becomes commercially available and even then there is no guarantee that it will prove a success.

Hybrid teas and floribundas

Hybrid tea and floribunda roses are bush roses. Hybrid teas (large-flowered bushes) produce large, normally full-centred, flowers in small numbers, whereas floribundas (cluster-flowered bushes) produce clusters of smaller flowers on each stem.

The hybrid teas are more popularly grown as their flowers are larger, on balance more beautiful and better scented. Their disadvantages are that their flowers do not stand up as well to wet weather as floribundas and, after a profusion of bloom in June, they only flower intermittently thereafter whereas floribundas flower almost continuously throughout the summer.

Choice is entirely subjective, although I have some recommendations, all of which have a good scent.

JULY

Here is my selection of hybrid-tea roses (average height 1m/3ft):

'Deep Scarlet'. Near-black buds opening to the darkest, richest red flowers.

'Dutch Gold'. Large, golden yellow flowers.

'Ena Harkness'. An old favourite, with large crimson flowers.

'Fragrant Cloud'. Large coral red flowers fading in hot weather.

'India Summer'. Pale orange flowers more resiliant to wet weather than most.

'Just Joey'. Large, coppery orange flowers with paler ends to the petals.

'Silver Jubilee'. Salmon-pink shaded with peach and coppery-pink.

'Summer Fragrance'. Large, deep red flowers.

'Super Star'. Bright vermilion flowers.

A selection of scented floribunda roses (average height 1m/3ft):

'Elizabeth of Glamis'. Orange-salmon flowers.

'English Miss'. Light pink flowers, edged with deeper pink.

'Fragrant Delight'. Coppery-salmon, yellow at base.

'Margaret Merril'. One of the most strongly scented of all the floribundas, with white flowers.

'Mountbatten'. Large, mimosa-yellow flowers.

'Queen Elizabeth'. Large, clear pink flowers.

'Sexy Rexy'. A dreadful name for a lovely rose with rose-pink flowers.

Rambling roses

Rambling roses enjoyed their heyday in Edwardian times and soon afterwards, during the first couple of decades of the twentieth century. Their popularity has since waned in favour of climbing roses, presumably because they only flower intermittently after their first flush of flower. This is a great shame as rambling roses perform a valuable role in the garden that no other rose can fulfil. They are so much

JULY

more graceful, less stiff, than climbing roses. They do need more space than climbing roses and are therefore ideally suited to being trained up trees, over large pergolas, up and over swagged chain or rope between poles and over buildings like garages or sheds and best left to take their own course. Here are a few I recommend:

All the following grow to a height of approximately 7.5m (25ft).
P = needs the protection of a sheltered position

'Albéric Barbier' P. Very vigorous, scented, creamy-white flowers
    with a lemon-yellow blush opening from yellow buds.
'Albertine'. Salmon red buds open to large, coppery pink, scented
    flowers. Very bushy and excellent for growing over a fence. Widely
    grown for very good reason.
Rosa arvensis (Field rose). An indigenous species with scented,
    single, white flowers, opening soon after our other native rambler
    R canina (Dog rose, pink flowers). Both have enormous charm
    mainly because of the simplicity of their flowers. Although most
    commonly seen growing in hedgerows, they too have a place in
    the garden.
Rosa banksiae banksiae (Banksian rose) P. Strongly scented, hanging
    sprays of small, white flowers in late May, early June. *R. b.*
    'Lutescens' has canary-yellow flowers. Choose your best, warmest
    wall for this beauty.
'Paul's Himalayan Musk'. Slightly scented, small, soft pink,
    rosette-like flowers beautifully arranged on graceful arching stems.
'Rambling Rector'. Well scented, semi-double, white flowers with
    showy yellow stamens.
Rosa wichuriana. Vigorous, with well-scented, small white flowers
later than most ramblers, in August.

Ground cover roses

Ground cover or 'procumbent' roses are useful for the front of the border where they grow into low cushions. They are not dense in growth and are not weed-supressors. Few have much scent.

'Pheasant', H75cm (2.5ft) S2.1m (7ft). Double, pink flowers.

'Red Blanket', H75cm (2ft 6in) S1.5m (5ft). Sprays of semi-double, red flowers. Repeat-flowering.

'Fairyland', H60cm (2ft) S1.5m (5ft). Small, pink, semi-double flowers.

'Magic Carpet', H75cm (30in) S120cm (4ft). Scented, lilac flowers.

'Suffolk', H45cm (18in) S1m (3ft). Single bright scarlet flowers. One of several named after counties, two others being 'Berkshire' (cherry pink) and 'Gwent' (clear yellow).

'Nozomi', H30cm (1ft) 1.5m S(5ft). Pearly pink flowers. A good subject for the rock garden.

Miniature roses

Perfectly scaled-down tiny roses, rarely grown these days in Britain (although they are popular in the USA). More's the pity as they make ideal plants for children's gardens, as well as in pots on tables on the terrace. Their height averages 30cm (1ft). Most are scentless. Some of the prettiest are:

'Cinderella'. White and pink very double flowers.

'Lavender Lace'. Lavender flowers. One of the few miniature roses with scented flowers.

'Snow Carpet'. Both a miniature and a ground cover rose, with very double, pure white flowers.

Rose hedges

The best roses to form hedges are those that are bushy in habit, so this excludes most of the hybrid teas and the floribundas, with the possible exception of white-flowering 'Iceberg'. While it is impossible

❧ JULY

to create a neat hedge, as is easily achieved with yew or beech, a shaggy rose hedge is a wonderful sight when in bloom and it also creates an impenetrable barrier. A mixed rose hedge sounds lovely, but it is not easy to keep one in a uniform shape as few roses grow at exactly the same rate and with the same habit. Rose hedges are best clipped back in spring with shears.

LARGE ROSE HEDGES

Species roses make the best rose hedges. The most important thing to remember about them is that they will need to be as wide as they are tall if the flowering performance is not to be reduced. The average height and spread of the following species roses 2m (6ft) or more. Plant 2m (6ft) apart.

Rosa hugonis (Golden rose of China). Soft yellow flowers in early summer and a lovely fern-like foliage for the rest of the season. One of the best roses of all for hedging.

Rosa moyesii. Blood-red flowers, followed by long, flagon-shaped, orange red hips from August to October.

Rosa eglanteria (Eglantine rose). Clear pink flowers followed by bright red, oval-shaped hips that last well into winter. Rich and spicy fragrant foliage.

Rosa rugosa 'Alba'. Although strictly not a species rose it was found as a sport on a *R. rugosa*. Slightly scented, large pure white flowers throughout the summer followed by large tomato-like, orange red hips.

MEDIUM-SIZED ROSE HEDGES

For smaller gardens, my choice of rose for a lower hedge are hybrid musks which can be clipped to about 120cm-2m (4-6ft) in height and width.

'Ballerina'. Large sprays of slightly scented, small, single pink flowers with white centres.

JULY

'Buff Beauty'. Strongly scented, rich apricot-yellow flowers
   throughout summer.
'Cornelia'. Large clusters of moderately scented, semi-double,
   apricot-pink blooms against a foil of bronzy foliage.
'Felicia'. Moderately scented, fully double pinky salmon flowers.
   Often referred to in text books as being the best of its group.
'Penelope'. Slightly scented, semi-double, creamy-pink flowers.

BURGLAR-PROOF HEDGE?

I wouldn't much like to have to walk through an established hedge of
any of the above, although the thorniest of all the roses is *R. sericea
pteracantha* whose decorative thorns are red, triangular and flat, measuring 20mm (³/₄in) at their base and are the plant's chief attraction
especially when the sun shines through them. The flowers are nothing
much to talk about, being white with four petals.

Where to plant roses

Formal island beds are those devoted to nothing but hybrid teas and
floribundas. They do not represent good value for most gardens as the
plants are mere prickly sticks for a good seven months of the year.
Soften an island bed with a surrounding dwarf box hedge.

   Integrate bush roses into different parts of the garden. They
always look at home in mixed borders or beds. Alternatively they can
be planted in the vegetable garden for picking.

Rose chores

PRUNING

The two most important things to remember when pruning roses is
always to prune back to an out-facing bud and to keep the centre of
the plant open to reduce attack of pests and diseases. Bush roses are
best cut back hard, reducing the bush by about two-thirds. Pruning
can take place in either autumn or spring, although the removal of

❧ JULY

top growth in November will help prevent the roots from suffering as a result of top growth being buffeted in winter winds.

DEAD-HEADING

Plants, like humans, have an inherent drive to procreate. By dead-heading roses once the flowers have faded you encourage them to repeat flower in order to produce more seed. However, some species of roses do not prove remontant.

REMOVING SUCKERS

Suckers are shoots growing from the rootstock (the roots onto which roses are grafted). If they are left to their own devices they will eventually take over. They are easily recognized as their leaves are smaller and lighter in colour than those of the grafted rose. They appear close to the base of roses and there is only one way to remove them. They must be traced back to the point of origin on the root, often involving excavation with a trowel and then gently torn or pulled off the root. If you cut them above ground, a common mistake, it merely makes things worse as the original single sucker then branches into a much stronger one.

PLANT PROPAGATION

Although in nature all plants reproduce themselves from seed, if they are hybrids, or if they fail to produce seed for some other reason, it becomes necessary to propagate them by various other means.

Cuttings

A cutting is a piece of a plant's stem, leaf or root, which is induced to form roots of its own so that it develops into a young plant identical to its 'parent'. Many plants can be propagated from cuttings, from hardy shrubs to greenhouse plants, but the type of cutting depends on the plant.

Cuttings of hardy shrubs, hardy herbaceous perennials and tender greenhouse plants such as begonia, coleus, fuchsia and tradescantia are all taken in the same way. Cuttings should be about 8cm (3in) long and should be cut cleanly just below a leaf joint. Remove the lower leaves close to the stem and dip the cuttings in hormone rooting powder or liquid. Do not allow the cuttings to dry out, have your small pots ready and make holes with a pencil-thin dibber. Plant the cuttings immediately, and firm them in. Make sure there are no air pockets by watering with a fine rose on the watering can.

Softwood cuttings are prepared from very soft young shoots early in the year, from April to June. They need plenty of warm, humid air in which to root. Enclose them in a polythene bag tied at the top and keep them on a warm well-lit window sill out of direct sunlight, or invest in an electrically heated propagating case.

Hardwood cuttings need no heat at all to root. They are taken in early and mid-winter. Current year's shoots which are ripe or woody are cut into 23-30cm (9-12in) lengths with sharp secateurs just above a bud at the top and just below at the base. Dip the base in hormone rooting powder and insert them up to two-thirds of their length in a V-shaped trench in a sheltered, well-drained spot outdoors. Firm them in well and they will be well rooted by the following autumn.

Root cuttings can be taken from such shrubs as rhus, sambucus, aralia and celastrus, trees such as ailanthus, catalpa, robinia and elm and hardy perennials like anchusa, echinops, border phlox and alpines. Root cuttings should be taken when the plants are dormant in mid-winter. Use young, slim roots. Scrape the soil away from large plants and removing a few roots, returning the soil and firming. The roots should be cut into 5cm (2in) sections with a sharp knife and planted vertically. The top of the cutting is always that part that was nearer the stem of the parent plant.

The cuttings can be rooted in pots or boxes containing a sandy medium in a cold frame or greenhouse. Top growth will be produced first, so give the cuttings time and do not lift them too early for planting out.

JULY

Division

This is the simplest way of propagating plants. In nature, plants must be able to survive accidents, so they have the ability to grow again when split into pieces.

Most herbacious perennials need lifting and dividing every three to four years to keep them vigorous. Many kinds of plants can be increased by division.

The best time to divide plants is early autumn to allow them to start to get their roots down before the winter sets in.

Lift clumps carefully with a fork, shake off the soil and discard the centre of the clump. Cut the outer, healthy parts of the plant, complete with roots, with a sharp spade and replant.

Perennials that flower early in the year should be divided immediately after flowering to give them time to settle into their new home during the growing season.

Bulbs and corms

Bulbs such as daffodil, tulip and hyacinth and corms such as crocus and gladiolus form secondary bulbs/corms around their bases. If the parent plants are dug up after the foliage has died down, these young bulbs/corms can be broken off and stored in a cool, dry place until they can be planted in the autumn — except gladiolus which is planted in mid to late spring. They should not be planted too deeply and will not flower for two to three years.

Layering

Many trees and shrubs can be propagated by layering, which involves pegging down a branch or shoot into the soil where it will form roots. Once it has become independent of the parent plant it can be detached and planted out. The best time to do this is in spring or early summer when plants are active. Prepare the ground by forking to

JULY

break it down and add plenty of moist peat and sand.

Choose young shoots or stems that bend easily down to the ground and cut with a sharp knife at a point about 30cm (12in) from the tip, with a sloping gash. Take a piece of wire bent to form a pin and peg the shoot down where it is wounded to a depth of about 7-8cm (3in). Cover with soil and firm it with your fingers. Keep the layers well watered. Some shrubs, such as lilac, forsythia, weigela and philadelphus, will form a good root system within a year; others, such as magnolia, witch hazel, rhododendron and azalea may take longer. When the layers have rooted, lift them carefully with a fork and cut them from the parent plant close to their new root. Plant the layers out immediately.

JULY TASKS

❀ Pour water onto the greenhouse floor to increase humidity. This prevents plants from suffering from leaf scorch.

❀ During dry spells it is best to raise the blades on the mower. This results in a greener lawn.

❀ In long, dry spells give recently planted trees and shrubs a good soaking.

❀ Summer-flowering shrubs that have outgrown their alloted space can be cut back once they have finished flowering.

❀ Water all containerized plants every day, even if it rains.

❀ Plant autumn-flowering crocus (*Colchicum*) around the base of deciduous trees for their welcome flowers in September and October.

❀ Keep the top on water butts to prevent the water from greening and the breeding of mosquitoes.

❀ Dead-head roses and dahlias regularly to promote a longer flowering season.

❀ Water newly planted climbers in dry weather to help them get their roots down.

❀ The foliage on fruiting vines and tomatoes can be cut out to allow the sun to get at the fruit.

JULY

❀ Pinch out flower spikes on Coleus, a plant grown for its ornamental foliage.

❀ Plant peonies and foxtail lilies in enriched soil to allow them to get their roots down before the winter. Divide congested clumps of hellebore.

❀ Choose a nice hot day to wash flower pots. This reduces the likelihood of transmission of disease.

❀ Formal hedges of Beech or Hornbeam can be cut this month or next. If you use an electric hedge trimmer, or any electrical appliance for that matter, make sure it is plugged into a circuit breaker, to avoid a nasty or even fatal accident.

❀ Continue to water tomatoes regularly. Irregular watering sometimes produces cracked fruits.

❀ Either remove altogether, or pot up strawberry runners for fresh young plants.

❀ New shoots on hybrid blackberries and loganberries will produce next year's fruit. Tie in a neat fan shape. Fruiting shoots must be cut out at ground level once all the fruit has been harvested.

❀ Protect dahlias from earwigs by trapping them in up-turned flower pots filled with straw on the top of bamboo canes. Every morning they can be tapped into a bucket of water.

❀ Make sure a friend or neighbour can come in when you are away on holiday to pick fruit and vegetables in season.

JULY ❀

High days and holidays

AUGUST

I T IS NOW A YEAR SINCE I STARTED writing my diary on the development of my garden. It has taught me a lot despite the fact that I am always designing gardens for other people – it is always different when it comes to your own. The only big change I have made is to reduce the amount of hedging in the large garden for reasons of budget. Sometimes it has felt as if I was taking two steps back every time I took one forward.

When I was studying horticulture at Merrist Wood in Surrey in 1976, I learnt the importance of knowing exactly where underground service pipes lay. Yet again I have punctured the mains water pipe, but then these pipes are not easy to find on old properties like this. A large wooden stake destined to support a raised section of my topiary garden at the front of the house hit the pipe fair and square. As it is so old, a whole section will have to be replaced and that means waiting for the plumber. I hate waiting for the plumber.

There's always plenty to do in August. Plants need staking and dead-heading and there is always a renegade weed. I have been cutting back summer-flowering shrubs like weigela and philadelphus, lifting and dividing early summer-flowering perennials and taking cuttings of zonal pelargoniums and osteospermums. This is also a good month for taking cuttings of all one's favourite shrubs.

There are very few wasps this year, but those that have appeared are dangerously sleepy – Alexandra stepped on one yesterday and it gave her a nasty sting on the sole of her foot. A friend of mine once got stung in the mouth by a wasp when mowing the lawn. The best thing to do with stings in the mouth is to suck ice to keep the swelling down and, if it is near to or in the throat, it is off to the hospital without delay. I hate wasps even more than I hate waiting for the plumber.

I have also been knocking a hole in the wall in the centre of the silver and white border in order to open up the vista from the new terrace through to the potager beyond. The gate posts are in but what about the gate? Gates are rather like human faces. They are either beautiful, plain or ugly. I want to achieve a gate that looks like a cobweb whose strands hang heavy with dew. The ever attentive spider must star, I think, face-on and in 3-D, but it is important that it looks like a spider's web. It has to be made, therefore, of the thinnest possible metal, but it must be practical. I await the detailed drawing and estimate.

I would have liked to have some nice old York paving outside the drawing room windows, but for budgetry reasons I have opted for a simulated concrete alternative made with a ridged, natural-looking finish. They are the closest I can find colourwise to my Cotswold stone. I have chosen 30cm (1ft) squares only and will lay them just as I have done with great success in bathrooms, using the cheapest possible white tiles (see illustration, page 36).

I have been adding and deleting from the silver and white border. I have added *Onopordum acanthium*, that wonderfully statuesque, silver, biennial thistle, but I shall have to turn a blind eye to its pink flowers that appear in mid-summer. I have dug out all the feverfew that so successfully filled the many gaps in this new border and they were more than adequately replaced by *Nicotiana sylvestris*, the most statuesque of all the flowering tobaccos, with long white hanging trumpets massed on the top of 180cm (6ft) stems. As I write on 23 August, the Japanese anemones 'Honorine Jobert' have only just started to flower and I still wait for my mildew-resistant Michaelmas Daisy (*Aster novae-angliae* 'Herbstschnee') to come into flower.

The more I garden the more I appreciate these plants that perform late in the season. I have reserved a special place at the base of a sunny wall for *Nerine bowdenii*, the Guernsey lily, that flowers in September and October. It is such a pity that its flowers are a brash ice-cream pink, but beggars cannot be choosers. It is the only reliably hardy species of Diamond lily to survive my cold, exposed garden.

One area of the property I haven't yet tackled surrounds the new conservatory on the end of what we call, very grandly, the East Wing. I had a pretty good idea of what the soil was like because when we moved in last year an enormous spreading sage was growing very happily there. That told me that the soil was probably quite poor, shallow and quick-draining and this was confirmed when I found the remains of an old cobbled yard, with the stones a mere six inches, if that, below gritty stone. Soon afterwards, I discovered the house's original well where I have now laid paving. It was in perfect condition, beautifully lined in stone and almost 20ft deep. In order to gain access to it, I have placed a paver with a metal ring in it over the top to blend in with the rest of the terrace.

The original sage that had spread out over the gravel covering an area of several square yards became so trampled that it had to be discarded, but another will be planted in its memory along with other aromatic xerophytic plants (those that like dry conditions) like rosemaries, lavenders, cotton lavenders, thymes and artemesias. I would have liked to have exposed the cobbled yard but there seem to be so many other more important things to do at the moment. Xeroscaping, landscaping using xerophytic plants, is big in the USA at the present time and becoming ever more popular over here too. No doubt as the reality of global warming makes itself felt on this side of the water it will become a neccessity rather than a mere fad. I saw a beautiful sight two days ago – *Artemesia* 'Powis Castle' covered in ladybirds. If just one silver sprig with two or three red ladybirds sitting on it were copied in the manner of Fabergé, it would make a beautiful brooch.

❧ AUGUST

DAY OF THE TRIFFIDS

Thinking of all the weeding that needs doing in the summer months makes me think of the two classic tales of plants being introduced from one continent to another, both with the most disastrous results. The first was Japanese knotweed (*Fallopia japonica*), introduced to Europe from Japan in the 1880s as a pretty, ornamental perennial and first noticed as a 'garden escapee' in 1886. It has since taken a stranglehold in many parts of the country and is difficult to eradicate because it has such a deep and strong root system.

The second escapee is the floating hyacinth (*Eichhornia crassipes*), a native of tropical Central America, which was introduced to India and then to Britain as an ornamental pond plant, since when it has spread into the open waterways and has succeeded in completely choking many of them.

MOVING POLICY

As well as moving plants that prove to be 'mistakes' where I have put them (see page 68), I also move plants that, for no apparent reason, do not do well in a certain position. I find that moving them to another part of the garden sometimes results in them taking on a new lease of life, with vigorous growth and plenty of flower. I give plants that do not seem to be thriving a couple of seasons in which to redeem themselves, after which I move them and hope for the best. Leaving them any longer may set them back as moving them then may damage their better-established root systems.

PLANTS FOR LATE SUMMER AND AUTUMN

It is in autumn that the garden can so easily look tired and devoid of colour. This is avoided by choosing plants that perform late on in the season to give that welcome splash of colour before winter (see also, winter pots page 157).

AUGUST ❀

Here is a selection of late-summer- and autumn-flowering shrubs:

H = eventual Height   S = eventual Spread   E = Evergreen
S/E = Semi-Evergreen

Abelia x *grandiflora* H3m (10ft) S4m (12ft) E. Compact, with arching
branches bearing scented pink-tinged flowers.
Aralia elata (Japanese angelica tree) 7.5 x 7.5m (24 x 24ft). A large
shrub or small tree with small white flowers, although the leaves
are its main attraction.
Ceanothus 'Autumnal Blue' E 3 x 3m (10 x 10ft). Sky-blue flowers.
Clerodendrum trichototum 5 x 5m (16 x 16ft). Scented white flowers
followed by bright blue berries.
Elaegnus x *ebbingei* 'Gilt Edge' E 4 x 4m (12 x 12ft). Dark green leaves
edged in golden yellow that last well into the autumn.
Eucryphia glutinosa H10m (30ft) S6m (20ft) S/E. A large shrub/small
tree with white flowers and good autumn tints.
Fatsia japonica 2-4 x 2-4m (6-12 x 6ft-12ft) E. Branched, creamy
white flowers and palmate leaves. An excellent sea-side plant.
Frcmontodcndron 'California Glory' (Flannel bush) H6m (20ft) S4m
(12ft). Large, yellow, waxy flowers from spring to autumn. One
of the longest flowering of all garden plants.
Fuchsia 'Mrs Popple' 1 x 1m (3 x 3ft). Scarlet and purple violet
flowers. Cut back hard in March.
Hibiscus syriacus 'Blue Bird' H3m (10ft) S2m (6ft). Large,
trumpet-shaped, light blue flowers with red centres. There are
several other varieties with flowers of different colours including
H. s. 'Diana' (pure white) and 'Woodbridge' (rich pink).
Hydrangea paniculata 'Tardiva' H5m (16ft) S2.5m (8ft). Large,
creamy-white flowers. Cut back hard in spring.
Lavatera 'Barnsley' 2 x 2m (6 x 6ft). White flowers ageing to soft
pink. Cut back hard in spring.
Mahonia x *media* 'Lionel Fortescue' H5m (16ft) S4m (12ft) E. Scented,
yellow flowers.

❈ AUGUST

Viburnum tinus 'Eve Price' H3 x 3m (10 x 10ft) E. Pink buds opening
   to white flowers.

Here are some climbers for late summer and autumn:

H = Approximate eventual Height

Clematis 'Bill MacKenzie' H6m (20ft). Bell-shaped, single
   yellow flowers.
Clematis flammula H6m (20ft). Star-shaped, scented white flowers.
Clematis 'Lady Betty Balfour' H3m (10ft). Purple-blue flowers with
   yellow anthers.
Clematis 'Gravetye Beauty' H2.5m (8ft). Rich crimson
   red flowers.
Eccremocarpus scaber (Chilean Glory Flower) H4m (13ft) E. Tubular,
   orange-red flowers. Needs the protection of a warm wall.
Lonicera periclymenum 'Graham Thomas' H7m (22ft). Strongly
   scented white flowers.
Magnolia grandiflora 'Exmouth' H6-18m (20-60ft) E. Large
   creamy white flowers.

And here are some late-summer-flowering herbaceous perennials for
the border:

Aster x *frikartii* 'Monch' H70cm (28in) S40cm (16in). Violet blue
   flowers with orange/yellow centres. One of the showiest of all the
   Michaelmas daisies.
Cimicifuga simplex 'Elstead' (Bugbane) H60-90cm (2-3ft) S60cm (2ft).
   Thin spires of white flowers.
Eupatorium rugosum (White snakeroot) H1.5m (5ft) S60cm (2ft).
   White flowers and nettle-like, fresh green leaves.
Helianthus salicifolius (Perennial sunflower) H2.5m (8ft). Golden
   yellow flowers with brown centres.
Helenium 'Sonnenwunder' H1.5m (5ft) S60cm (2ft). Masses of yellow

AUGUST ❧

flowers with brownish centres. The perennial heleniums are invaluable for late summer and autumn, with many other varieties with dirty red, orange or dirty yellow flowers.

Hosta plantaginea (Plantain lily) H30cm (1ft) S1m (3ft). Scented white flowers.

Liriope muscari H30cm (1ft) S45cm (18in) E. Spikes of violet-blue flowers and strap-like flowers. A very tough plant, useful for growing under the outer canopy of evergreen trees.

Ophiogon planiscapus var. *nigrescens* ('Black Dragon') H20cm (8in) S30cm (12in). Purplish white flowers contrast with nearly black leaves.

Leucanthemella serotina H1.5m (5ft) S1m (3ft). White, daisy-like flowers with green/yellow centres.

Rudbeckia maxima H1.2m (4ft) S60cm (2ft). The most striking of the rudbeckias, with golden yellow petals and a large black cone at the centre.

Sedum spectabile (Ice plant) 45 x 45cm (18 x 18 in). Pink flowers that are very attractive to bees.

Schizostylis coccinea (Kaffir lily) H60cm (2ft) S30cm (1ft). Sword-shaped leaves and small gladiolus-like scarlet flowers.

OUTDOOR FURNITURE

August is usually the hottest time in Britain and a marvellous time for eating out with family and friends, either in a shaded place at midday or on a warm, balmy evening. Finding furniture that looks right in the garden and is also comfortable is so important. There's nothing like eating outside; somehow the food tastes all the better. Table and chairs spread under the canopy of a mature tree is an achievable dream for many.

Garden furniture can prove to be one of the most expensive items in a garden. There is an enormous marketplace out there groaning with benches, tables, chairs, swing hammocks and what have you made in a wide range of materials and so the choice is bewilderingly large.

❧ AUGUST

The most expensive material is teak, a hardwood which, with age, takes on a silver sheen. Cheaper, widely available wood garden furniture is made of softwood, normally pine. Average-price, softwood wooden furniture will last a great many years if treated regularly with wood preservative and brought in under cover every winter. You can buy excellent copies of classical stone seats which, like new statuory, can be 'antiqued'. Moulded PVC furniture has taken the market by storm. This is hardly surprising as it is comfortable and cheap.

Whatever you choose it can be designed into the garden in a number of different ways. Wherever possible garden furniture should never look 'plonked'. Here are some ideas:

❀ Place a seat to face the best views of the garden, or views beyond if you're lucky enough to have them.
❀ Have a bench at the focal point of a garden as a vista-stopper (see page 9). A white-painted bench will stand out all the more.
❀ Create an arbour of scented climbing plants. A simple arbour can be built using trellis panels. As you sit in the comfort of the shade supplied by the climbers, scent wafts all around as you admire the garden.
❀ A shaded bench close to the house, facing east, is perfect for outside breakfasts in the cool sun and teas and suppers in the shade when the sun is much hotter.
❀ Consider a swing hammock or bench.

A shaded table

Shade is important for summer. I have had an idea that I want to try to achieve in my garden, although I have never actually seen it done. You can create your own living parasol by training a Portuguese laurel (*Prunus lusinatica*) into a mushroom shape. This will take a number of years, but once the mushroom shape has been achieved a removable round table can be fixed into place. This consists of two semi-circles on collapsible legs that can be slotted together, with a

AUGUST ❀

small central semi-circular hole cut into each to accommodate the tree trunk. It is ideas like this that make gardens special.

My idea for a garden table with a living parasol.

TIP: MOWING

Benches on lawns should always be placed on paving so that they do not have to be moved when mowing.

AGEING TRICK

New pots, urns, statues and seats, the sort made of reconstituted cement, can all be treated to give them a patina of age. They can be daubed with a thick slurry, the consistency of porridge, of peat substitute and full fat milk or yoghurt, in dry weather. The end result is that the stone is darkened and will, with any luck, eventually attract algae and lichens. However, you will be more likely to get lichens if you live in an area where the air is not polluted.

Sir Clough Williams-Ellis, the creator of Portmeirion in Wales, used to collect carvings from buildings due for demolition. His technique for ageing these carvings was to bury them in the ground.

AUGUST

COLLECTING SEEDS

The seed of many garden plants can be collected for re-sowing the following spring, the financial benefits of which are very attractive. Only the seeds of true wild plants produce offspring identical to the parent plant. Man-bred cultivars, often referred to as F1 hybrids, will produce mixed seedlings with few if any being exactly the same as the parent. However, that's not to say you shouldn't collect these seeds, as you may be pleasantly surprised by the outcome.

The time to collect seeds is before they ripen, just before the seed capsule releases them. This is normally late summer or early autumn.

To collect and store seeds safely: tie a paper bag around the seed heads to catch them; put the collected seed into labelled paper bags, envelopes or linen bags, then into a biscuit tin or other airtight container; store them in a cool, dry, frost-free place.

There are several plants that do the sowing for you. Always leave one or two seed heads when dead-heading any of the following plants, to allow them to scatter their seeds themselves.

These are all annuals unless otherwise stated.
P = Perennial B = Biennial,

Alchemilla mollis (Lady's mantle) P H60cm (2ft) S75cm (30in). Yellow flowers ideal for drying and pale green leaves that catch raindrops.

Digitalis (Foxglove) B H1m (3ft) S30cm (1ft). Spires of magic purple flowers. There are varieties with flowers of white, pink and many other shades.

Erigeron karvinskianus 'Profusion' (Fleabane) P H30cm (1ft) S50cm (20in). This is a special plant, covered in masses of tiny, pink and white, small daisy-like flowers all summer, capable of growing in the meanest crack or crevice on vertical and horizontal surfaces.

Limnanthes douglasii (Poached-egg plant) 15 x 15cm (6 x 6in). Cushions of yellow-centred white flowers in May. Completely disappears by summer.

AUGUST

Lunaria annua 'Alba Variegata' (Variegated honesty) H60cm (2ft) S30cm (1ft). White flowers and leaves splashed generously in white, followed by flat, silvery seed pods. So much more rewarding than plain honesty with purple flowers and plain green leaves, although it loses its decorativeness soon after flowering and is therefore best tucked away behind a later-flowering herbaceous perennial.

Myosotis sylvatica (Forget-me-not) H30cm (1ft) S15cm (6in). Seas of rich, pale-blue flower in spring and early summer. Perfect for the wild garden where it will grow in amongst grass.

Nicandra physalodes (Apple of Peru) H60cm (2ft) S30cm (1ft). Violet-blue, bell-shaped flowers with a white throat and toothed leaves covered in tiny, pin-prick-sized, black dots.

Nicotiana alata (Tobacco plant) H1.5m (5ft) S30cm (1ft). Strongly scented white flowers in the evening and at night.

Nigella damascena (Love-in-a-mist). Pale blue flowers surrounded by a fine ruffle.

Onopordium acanthium (Scotch thistle) B H3m (10ft), S1m (3ft). Sculptural silver leaves and pale purple or white flowers in July and August. A statuesque giant.

Papaver somniferum (Opium poppy) H1m (3ft) S30cm (1ft). Handsome silvery foliage with white, red or purple, single or double flowers in June and July.

Viola cornuta 'Alba' (Horned violet) H30cm (1ft) S45cm (18in). Masses of small, white flowers in a neat cushion mound. Best cut right back in July for a second flush of flower.

COUNTRY OF ORIGIN

One of the best pieces of advice I can give to anyone, and *the* most important thing to do before making a decision to plant anything you are not certain of, is to find out a plant's 'natural distribution' – its country of origin and the sort of conditions it grows under in that country. The majority of garden plants, ranging from huge trees to tiny alpines, have been introduced to this country from other continents as well as more southern parts of Europe, mainly since the sixteenth century, and they need to be cultivated accordingly. To choose an obvious example, it would be a waste of time and money trying to grow a *Passiflora racemosa*, a beautiful passion flower with red flowers, in an open position in a frost pocket in Essex, as it enjoys scrambling through vegetation in the much warmer climate of Rio de Janeiro, Brazil. Few books mention plants' country of origin, although the *New RHS Dictionary of Gardening*, published by Macmillan, does.

AUGUST TASKS

❊ In dry spells remember to water the leaves of evergreens as well as the roots.

❊ *Nerine bowdenii* (Guernsey lily) can be watered and fed if the soil is very dry to give it a boost for flowering in early autumn.

❊ Keep ferns well watered. They resent a parched soil.

❊ Herbaceous perennials that have finished flowering can be lifted and divided where they have become over-congested.

❊ Sow a last crop of lettuce as well as spring cabbage.

❊ In dry weather mow without a collecting box. Clippings that fall back onto the lawn will add nitrogen to the soil.

❊ Plant forced hyacinth bulbs in bowls for Christmas flowering. Order or buy spring flowering bulbs without delay.

❊ Take cuttings of osteospermums for bedding plants next summer.

❊ Trim back faded flowers on cotton lavender (*Santolina*) with shears back to the top leaves.

❊ Cut back all raspberry canes that have finished fruiting down to the ground.

❊ Michaelmas daisies, now heavy with flowers, may need supporting.

❊ Carrots will need to be harvested before they become too woody and tasteless.

❊ Collect and dry the seeds of fennel and dill and divide congested clumps of chives.

Index